The Joy of Swearing

The Joy of Swearing

M. Hunt

with Alison Maloney

Michael O'Mara Books Limited

First published in Great Britain in 2006 by
Michael O'Mara Books Limited
9 Lion Yard
Tremadoc Road
London SW4 7NQ

A CIP catalogue record for this book is available from the British Library

ISBN (10 digit): 1-84317-162-7
ISBN (13 digit): 978-1-84317-162-1

1 3 5 7 9 10 8 6 4 2

www.mombooks.com

Designed and typeset by Design 23

Printed and bound in Great Britain by Cox & Wyman, Reading, Berks

I Thank You

With thanks to Andy Dougan and Rob Driscoll for their help and friendship. Thanks to Rod Green and Chris Maynard at Michael O'Mara Books and Sue Clark in the BBFC Press Office for the useful information. Last, but never least, thanks to Jim for his patience and support.

Contents

Introduction 9

Blue Blood, Blue Language 11

Famous Foul-mouths: Unparliamentary Language 24

Bleeping Broadcasting 31

Famous Foul-mouths: Song Sung Blue 53

Literary Language 57

Famous Foul-mouths: Celebrity Chefs 76

Big (Blue) Screen 81

Famous Foul-mouths: Actors Behaving Badly 96

Lyrical Language 103

Famous Foul-mouths: Sporty but Naughty 116

Filthy Wordplay 127

Famous Foul-mouths: No Laughing Matter 138

Fucking Fascinating Facts 145

Conclusion 158

Sources 160

Introduction

If you are easily shocked then now is the time to put down this book and walk away. From here on in, every page bears witness to a wide variety of oaths, curses, blasphemies and profanities that some may find offensive. Yet, everybody swears. Whether your favourite expletive is 'Damn!', 'Blimey!', Archibald Haddock's famous 'Billions of blue blistering barnacles' or a fully-fledged 'Fuck!', we all feel the urge to swear on occasion. Let's face it, if you happen to drop a rock on your foot while in polite company, it takes every ounce of self-control to stick to a harmless 'Bother!' – and you'd have to be a saint in this day and age to practice such linguistic control!

In 1821 William Hazlitt observed that 'the English . . . are a rather foul-mouthed nation.' It was ever thus. From the bawdy language and blasphemous oaths of Chaucer to the barely concealed smut of Shakespeare, throughout history we have continued to revel in filth. However, time has changed our 'appreciation' of various invectives; certain words have grown into acceptance, while others have fallen out of use, and, likewise, the places where such words can be used has changed as well. These days, as Cole Porter said, 'anything goes'. From literature to lyrics, stage to screen, politics to sport, no medium is safe from the advance of the invective.

Lady Chatterley, Eliza Doolittle, Quentin Tarantino and even the charming Hugh Grant have all taken up arms in battle against the tyranny of taboo. So, let us celebrate then, with them, the love of language less savoury; let us revel in rudeness and delight in dirty words, and join with me as we journey through *The Joy of Swearing*.

Blue Blood, Blue Language

Throughout history, and from the time the first exasperation, disappointment or fear struck a sovereign brow, the courts, palaces, castles and country houses of royals and aristocrats have rung with their fair share of oaths. Henry VIII and Elizabeth I were renowned for their colourful language, while in modern times Prince Philip, Princess Anne and Prince Charles have both been known to utter the odd obscenity. I'm pretty sure Prince Harry has a few up his sleeve too!

Elizabeth I

Although many people who lived during the reign of Elizabeth I sought to outlaw swearing (and other such personal proclivities deemed immoral), the Queen herself was no prude. When it came to the censorship of stage plays, Elizabeth was firmly on the side of free expression and, practising what she preached, was said to have sworn 'like a man'. A bill against 'usual and common swearing' failed to make it through the House of Lords in 1601 and Sir Francis Drake observed that 'a shocking practice seems to have been rendered fashionable by the Queen . . . for it is said that she never spared an oath in public speech or private conversation when she thought it added energy to either.' 'God's wounds!', which was said to have been her favourite phrase, may not sound shocking today, but it would certainly have had an impact on the upper-crust circles in the sixteenth-century court. (see 'zounds' on page 128).

Well known as a wit, Elizabeth used her language, foul or otherwise, to great advantage. In his *Brief Lives* (1693), John Aubrey recalls the tale of an eminent Earl, Edward de Vere, who passed wind while bowing to the Queen. Mortified by his faux pas, the Earl went travelling for seven years so as to get over his shame. On his return, it is said that Queen Elizabeth welcomed him home with the immortal words: 'My Lord, I had forgott the fart.'

Charles II and John Wilmot, second Earl of Rochester

It was around the time of the reign of Charles II (from 1665 to 1700) that plays, books and poems began to include words that many wouldn't have dared to utter when Cromwell and his Puritanical forces were running the country. One of the most celebrated wits in Charles's circle was John Wilmot, Lord Rochester, a writer and notorious libertine, whose language must have shocked even the most liberal of courtiers. He produced probably the dirtiest and raciest works ever written thus far, and eventually, for his pains, was banished from court by the King. In his poem 'A Satire on Charles II' he wrote:

> *I the Isle of Britain, long since famous growne*
> *For breeding the best cunts in Christendome*

Similarly, his innocuously titled poem 'A Ramble in Saint James's Parke', contains a multitude of swear words and sexual references.

> *Much wine had past with grave discourse*
> *Of who fucks who and who does worse*

> *But tho Saint James has the Honor on't*
> *'Tis consecrate to Prick and Cunt*

George V

King George V is best known for swearing on his deathbed. As he lay in bed at Sandringham House, Norfolk, surrounded by his family and close to death, the King's physician said, rather inaccurately, 'Your Majesty will soon be well enough to visit Bognor.'

The King, it is said, replied, 'Bugger Bognor,' and promptly died.

In order to spare the feelings of the nation, and particularly those of the residents of Bognor Regis, *The Times* reported his final words as, 'How is the Empire?' In this way, the nation was left with the comforting belief that the King's dying thought was for the kingdom.

However, a different account has the last words of the King as 'God damn you!' – a reaction, apparently, to his last shot of morphine being administered. 'Bugger Bognor' has a much better ring to it, though!

Prince Philip – the Duke of 'Edinbugger'

Never known for his tact or diplomacy, Prince Philip, Duke of Edinburgh, is said to be prone to four-letter outbursts. According to a recent article in *The Guardian*, a young, well-bred reporter covering the yachting events at Cowes Week on the Isle of Wight in the sixties went 'quite pale with the shock' of being told to 'fuck off' by the Duke of Edinburgh.

In 1983, the Queen and Prince Philip visited the United States as guests of former President Ronald Reagan and his wife Nancy. The royal visit began peacefully enough with the royal couple sitting in the back of a limousine in San Francisco. However, the Prince became increasingly impatient while waiting for Reagan's car to move away and begin the ceremonial motorcade. Philip asked his chauffeur to 'move the bloody car', and when the driver refused he screamed, 'Move this fucking car!' while hitting the poor unfortunate man across the back of his head with a magazine. The Queen, dignity intact, ignored the whole thing and gazed ahead silently.

Prince Charles

As far as we know Charles is not as fond as his father of the F-word but, somewhat appropriately for a fan of blood sports, he prefers the word 'bloody' to express his emotions. In 1982, appalled by the standard of English in his office, he fumed, 'English is taught so bloody badly!' When his 2005 skiing holiday with his sons was interrupted for the traditional press photograph, the peeved Prince was heard to mutter 'bloody people' before insulting the BBC's royal correspondent Nicholas Witchell. On a tour of Australia later that year he was asked by war veteran Gary Johnston for an invitation to his forthcoming wedding to Camilla Parker Bowles and, laughing, Charles replied, 'There's no bloody room . . . there's not enough bloody room.'

Prince Andrew

In 2003, *Daily Mirror* journalist Ryan Parry went undercover in Buckingham Palace by getting himself a job as a footman. Among the many things he revealed about the everyday lives of the Royals was that Prince Andrew did not like to be woken too early in the morning and that any footman brave enough to pull his curtains back risk being greeted with the words 'fuck off'.

Princess Anne

Perhaps the most famous incident of swearing from our current royal family was the transgression of Princess Anne in 1982. As press photographers attempted to take her picture during a difficult moment with her steed at the Badminton Horse Trials, she allegedly told them all to 'naff off'. The phrase was all over the newspapers the following morning.

The Royal Killjoys and the History of Censorship

For every foul-mouthed monarch, there is a stately stuffed shirt.

When warrior-king Henry V led his campaign in France, in 1415, discipline was so strict that swearing and blaspheming was strictly forbidden. His son, Henry VI, was said to be so pious that his worst curse was 'By St John!' which, even by fifteenth-century standards, was not exactly shocking.

After the reign of the mouthy monarch, Elizabeth I, things began to look increasingly bleak for the lovers of the profane. The influence of the Puritans was growing and, in 1606, during the reign of James I, a law was passed preventing any blasphemy or profanity in a stage play, with a fine of ten pounds imposed for each offence. This was followed by a ban on swearing in general, which came into force in 1623 and read thus:

For as much as all profane swearing and cursing is forbidden by the Word of God, be it therefore enacted, by the authority of the then parliament. That no person or persons should thenceforth profanely swear or curse, upon penalty of forfeiting one shilling to the use of the poor for every oath or curse.

Did this decree institute the world's first national swear box? Anyone who couldn't or wouldn't pay was subjected to time in the stocks or, if under the age of twelve, whipped.

The crackdown on swearing in public life had a twofold effect. The first was the proliferation of 'minced oaths'; those utterances that disguised traditional blasphemies as seemingly harmless language. Among the oaths that were shortened or disguised were ''snails' (from 'God's nails'), ''sfoot' (from 'God's foot') and 'zounds' (from 'God's wounds'). Shakespeare used the terms ''sblood' (predictably, 'God's blood') in *Henry IV, Part 1*, and ''slid' ('God's eyelid') in *The Merry Wives of Windsor*.

The second effect of the decree was that the source of invective language shifted from having a religious base to a secular one. Shakespeare has Pistol, the old soldier in *Henry V*, use terms such as 'cur', 'hound', 'braggart' and 'tike', but largely refrains from giving him the blasphemous insults that had been more prevalent in earlier literary works.

The rise of the Puritans culminated in the English Civil War and the succession to power of Oliver Cromwell in 1653. Cromwell was a devoutly religious man for whom the Bible's teachings were, literally, gospel. Puritans were so-called because of their adherence to the overarching authority and 'purity' of the Bible (as opposed to the Catholic heritage of superfluous creeds, rites and doctrines – as they saw it) – the result being that the Puritans attempted to suppress any forms of entertainment and the arts. Cromwell shut down theatres and inns, banned most sports and outlawed boys playing football on Sundays.

His stance on swearing was about as tough as it gets. Profanity was punishable with a fine or imprisonment, but his threat that 'not a man swears but pays his twelve pence' seems positively tame compared to the punishment meted out to one man in particular. A quartermaster found guilty under military law of uttering blasphemous expressions had his tongue bored through with a red-hot iron and a sword broken over his head before what was left of him was discharged from the service.

Around this time the production of pamphlets and publications decrying the sin of swearing was prolific. In 1645 Vicar Walter Powell published a 384-page diatribe entitled *A Summon For Swearers And A Law For The Lips In Reproving Them*, in which 'The Chief Dissuasives From Swearing Are Proposed, Strange Judgements Upon Swearers Related, Which May Be A Terror For The Wicked, Preservative For The Godly.' A scientist, Robert Boyle (he of Boyle's Law) attacked the use of 'minced oaths' in his 'A Free Discourse Against Customary Swearing; And, A Dissuasive From Cursing', published in 1695. Those who used 'fictitious terms and abbreviatures', he said, did not deceive God. 'Well may this childish evasion cheat our own souls, but never Him.'

However, and perhaps inevitably, a movement against such moral purity began to grow, and the period of the Restoration, from 1660 onwards, saw a reactionary rise in the lewdness, licentiousness and frivolity suppressed during Cromwell's rule – perhaps best exemplified by Lord Rochester, mentioned above. John Aubrey's *Brief Lives* typifies the language of the time when he writes of his contemporary, John Selden (a renowned scholar and barrister), that he'd 'got more by his Prick than his practise'.

Prudery began to creep back into society by the mid-eighteenth century, and by the beginning of the nineteenth century – the Regency period – profanity was once again frowned upon in polite circles. But it was to be the reign of Queen Victoria, from 1837 to 1901, which became renowned for its delicate sensibilities and strict code of conduct, including a renewed clampdown on swearing. Victorian gentlemen never swore in the presence of ladies, and the mildest of profanities was apt to make society ladies swoon. By and large, writers of the day avoided foul language and even the word 'damned' was viewed with the utmost horror. In Anthony Trollope's novel, *The Prime Minister,* one character utters the word in front of his young wife and Trollope explains, 'It was to her a terrible outrage . . . The word had been uttered with all its foulest violence, with virulence and vulgarity. It seemed to the victim to be the sign of a terrible crisis in her early married life.' Indeed, 'damn' has had a tough ride through history – see the controversy it provoked in Hollywood in the late thirties (page 83).

Although his characters moved among the cripplingly poor and the villains of Victorian society, Charles Dickens also steered clear of strong words, using expressions like 'jiggered' or 'drat' on the occasions when an expletive was called for. In *Nicholas Nickleby* he uses the word 'dem'd' ['damned'], and in *The Pickwick Papers* he replaces 'damned' with 'somethin' unpleasanted'.

As will be shown in the case of Mrs Beeton (see page 73), it wasn't even felt acceptable to say 'trousers' in front of a lady from the upper echelons of society. In *Oliver Twist,* the butler of the Maylie household, Giles, describes being awoken in the middle of the night.

> *'I tossed off the clothes,' said Giles, throwing away the table-cloth, and looking very hard at the cook and the housemaid, 'got softly out of bed; drew on a pair of—'*
> *'Ladies present, Mr Giles,' murmured the tinker.*
> *'—Of shoes, sir,' said Giles . . . '*

This intolerance of foul language throughout the Victorian era meant that the first half of the twentieth century saw, in most circles, no more than a moderate amount of swearing. In 1914, for instance, the word 'bloody' was still able to cause a national scandal when used on the West End stage (see pages 66-7). In 1936, the poet and novelist Robert Graves wrote:

Of recent years in England there has been a noticeable decline of swearing and foul language and this, except at centres of industrial depression, shows every sign of continuing indefinitely until a new shock to our national nervous system – envisageable as war, pestilence, revolution, fire from Heaven or whatever you please – may (or may not) revive the habit of swearing with that of praying.

Although there hasn't been much of a revival in the habit of praying, Graves's prediction was half right. The popularity of many swear words in use today can indeed be traced back to war. In both the UK and the US, the Second World War saw the most taboo words of the twentieth century unleashed with a vengeance, and a 'Pandora's box' of language opened. As language expert Eric Partridge observed, 'War is the greatest excitant of vocabulary' and, frankly, who can blame soldiers under fire for uttering the odd expletive?

The latter part of the twentieth century has seen the boundaries of what is acceptable in swearing shift dramatically. Today, the shackles of the Victorian era have hardly left a mark. Swearing is present in everyday conversation on the street or in the office, in books, on television programmes, in plays and in songs. If we see a Hollywood film without a single swear word, it's probably a Disney cartoon.

The Future of Swearing

As a nation we have become almost immune to traditional swear words. Recent surveys show that the words that were once taboo no longer offend the majority of people (with the possible exception of the C-word), and that the biggest taboo of the twenty-first century is racial abuse and of terms relating to race.

However, history has demonstrated that society can swing to and fro in its acceptance – and then its consequent rejection – of modes of expression, and profanity is no exception. Some recent news stories have suggested there could still be a backlash against the blanket acceptance of public swearing.

In April 2005, for example, the residents of an estate in Brighton took the exceptional step of banning swearing in public. New tenants on the Hollingdean estate are required to sign a contract agreeing not to use foul language in the street, and anyone who does not comply with this edict faces losing their home.

'People get quite distressed by groups of mainly young people who hang around shops and other public areas swearing loudly,' said Gill Mitchell, the local council's spokeswoman for the environment.

'We're not talking about someone cursing because they have dropped their wallet, but it is intimidating if you are standing at the bus stop where a group of people are swearing, often exacerbated by drink.'

A month later, Bluewater shopping centre in Kent hit the news when it banned not only people wearing 'hoodies' but swearing, too. Backed by Prime Minister Tony Blair and Deputy Prime Minister John Prescott, the centre said that anyone breaking the rules on antisocial behaviour would be escorted from the premises.

So is it possible that, in fifty or a hundred years' time, swearing will, once more, be driven underground? Watch this space.

Derivation: 'Fuck'

1: Fuck
a) verb – to copulate; to have sexual intercourse
b) noun – the act of sexual intercourse
c) noun – a sexual partner

2: Fucking
a) noun – as in 'a good fucking'
b) verb – as in 'fucking up'
c) adjective – as in 'a fucking bastard'
d) adverb – as in 'he fucking did it'

Often referred to as 'Anglo-Saxon' language, the origin of this well-known and versatile word is the subject of many myths and legends.

One story has it that the word derives from around the sixteenth and seventeenth centuries when the Puritan movement held England in its grip. The sin of fornication, or sexual intercourse outside of marriage, was punishable by being sent to the stocks, whipped, ostracized and other pretty harsh treatment. It is said that some offenders had to wear a placard with the words 'For Unlawful Carnal Knowledge' – F.U.C.K. – for short. In fact, 'unlawful carnal knowledge' is still an offence in the UK today. Another, very similar theory, was that it stood for 'Forced Unlawful Carnal Knowledge' and that rapists had an abbreviation of this crime branded on their forehead. These are both nonsense.

A third legend originates from the seventeenth century, around the time Britain was facing another plague. As so many were dying, a royal decree was issued telling all citizens to 'Fornicate Under Command of the King'. This was soon shortened to produce the verb, 'to fuck'.

All of these theories are neat and much more fascinating than the truth but, in fact, the word was around long before both the plague and the Puritan movement, which clearly invalidates both etymologies.

The origin of the English word is actually Germanic, from the Old German *ficken* or *fucken* meaning 'to strike or penetrate'. Experts believe these words were related to the Latin words for 'puncture' and 'prick', or to the Latin *futuere*, which is slang for 'to copulate'. Similar words in other parts of Europe include the Dutch *fokken*, meaning 'thrust' or, when applied to cattle, 'copulate or breed'. In Sweden, *focka* has the same meaning as 'fuck' in English and the Norwegian version is *fukka*. It is thought that the earliest uses of the word in English came via Scotland in the fifteenth century, although records from as early as 1278 identify the existence of a man called John Le Fucker (but he couldn't help that!).

A poem satirizing the Carmelites (a medieval monastic order) and written between 1450 and 1475 appears to feature the first recorded instance of the word. Although 'Feln flyys' is written in a complex mixture of English and Latin, it appears to use the term 'fuccant' as a pseudo-Latin term, though it's hidden in a code as even at this time the word evidently appears to have been a profanity. The passage in question refers to the monks, and translates as 'They are not in heaven, because they fuck the wives of Ely.'

By the late sixteenth century 'fuck' had become a widely used, if vulgar, term. It appeared in a dictionary, John Florio's *A World of Words*, in 1598.

Changing attitudes to swearing drove the word from polite society and respectable literature in the late nineteenth and early twentieth century, but it seemed to enjoy a resurgence during the Second World War, particularly as the basis of various military acronyms. 'FUBBED' meant 'Fucked Up Beyond Belief'; 'FUBAR', 'Fucked Up Beyond All Recognition'; 'FUNDY', 'Fucked Up, Not Dead Yet' (reportedly used in the hospital notes of injured soldiers); and 'SNAFU', 'Situation Normal, All Fucked Up' (see 'Naff off', page 132). More recent acronyms include 'NFW', meaning 'No Fucking Way' and 'NFG', which stands for 'No Fucking Good'. Also, a 'cluster fuck' is an almighty collection of things fucking up.

The joy of the word 'fuck' and all its variations is that it can be used in almost any part of a sentence as noun, adverb and adjective. Hence the perfectly grammatical phrase 'The fucking fucker's fucking fucked!' which has been attributed to a classics master at Eton swearing at his bicycle, an Irish farmer at his tractor, an Army truck driver at his truck and an actor at his broken shoelace in a high-speed scene change. The chances are that this beautifully constructed sentence has been used in all those situations and is destined to grace a few more in the future!

Variations include: fucked, fucking, fucker, fuck-up, fuckwit, fuck off, fuck me, fuck about, fuck someone about (or 'around' or 'over'), fuck something up, fuck-a-duck, fuck you, for fuck's sake, etc., etc.

Famous Foul-mouths: Unparliamentary Language

In the corridors of power in the UK and across the world, insults and profanities are frowned upon. In Britain, the use of so-called 'unparliamentary language' can result in the Speaker of the House demanding a retraction of the ill-phrased utterance, asking the potty-mouthed politican to leave the session, or suspending the offending representative from the Chamber for up to five days.

Words to which objection has been taken by the Speaker over the years include 'blackguard', 'coward', 'git', 'guttersnipe', 'hooligan', 'rat', 'swine', 'stoolpigeon' and 'traitor'. Nothing too racy there, perhaps.

While serving as Education Secretary in 2000, David Blunkett got into a bitter debate with Conservative backbencher David Tredinnick about education standards. Blunkett suggested that the Conservatives' policy on literacy, when they were in office, was 'to do sod all'. Mr Blunkett quickly realized he was in trouble and pre-empted the Deputy Speaker's reaction by withdrawing his comments 'as entirely unparliamentary language – and I have corrected myself'.

On another occasion in 1992, Dennis Skinner, dubbed 'the beast of Bolsover', called Minister for Agriculture John Gummer a 'wart' and a 'little squirt of a minister'. After refusing to retract the statement he was asked to leave the Commons Chamber for the rest of the day.

No matter how heated a debate becomes, swearing, even mildly, is not an option unless you want your knuckles rapped. Outside the chamber, however, there are a few politicians who have demonstrated the most unparliamentary of language.

Harry S. Truman

The President of the United States from 1945 to 1952, Truman was the son of a farmer from Missouri and was, apparently, fond of a little 'agricultural language' himself. Truman's wife, Bess, once commented that 'he liked to call horse manure, horse manure' and revealed that it had been hard to get him to use the polite version of this expression. On the sacking of General Douglas MacArthur from his role in Korea in 1951, he explained, 'I fired MacArthur because he wouldn't respect the authority of the President. I didn't fire him because he was a dumb son of a bitch, although he was.' He also referred to Richard Nixon as 'a no-good lying bastard.'

Lyndon B. Johnson

The thirty-sixth President of the United States, Lyndon Baines Johnson succeeded John F. Kennedy after Kennedy's assassination in 1963. Johnson was renowned for his love of profanity and, shockingly for the straight-laced America of the sixties, didn't tone his language down even in the presence of ladies. But he had a way with words and was pretty quick with a witty putdown.

Describing Gerald Ford he said, 'He is so dumb that he can't fart and chew gum at the same time.' And, on hearing a speech by Richard Nixon, it is claimed he said, 'I may not know much, but I know chicken shit from chicken salad.'

Richard Nixon

Richard Milhous Nixon was raised as an evangelical Quaker by his mother, Hannah, who hoped he would become a missionary. His family followed a strict Quaker lifestyle, banning drinking, dancing, and, of course, swearing, and Nixon often referred to his mother as a 'Quaker saint'. Unfortunately, her little boy wasn't quite as saintly himself.

The thirty-seventh President of the United States (from 1969 to 1974), Republican Nixon found himself in hot water when it was discovered that five burglars had broken into the Democratic offices in the Watergate complex, in Washington D.C., shortly before Nixon won a landslide victory in the 1972 election. The burglars were trying to install bugging devices and steal documents and, after the event, Nixon attempted a 'cover-up' of his involvement.

Unfortunately, Nixon had taped all the conversations that had taken place in his Oval Office. When the burglaries were revealed and the cover-up hit the headlines, Nixon tried to stop these tapes being released and, when he was subpoenaed to do so, released edited versions with all the swear words removed. While somewhat tame by today's standards, the public were still shocked by the amount of bleeps on the edited tapes. He called one particular news summary a 'bunch of crap' and, when talking about the informant known as 'Deep Throat', he commented, 'I know what I'd do with him, the bastard.'

Other favourite profanities used constantly by Nixon and his advisers were 'damn', 'Goddamn', 'Jesus', 'Christ', and 'shit'.

His love of the profane was indicated even before he entered the White House when, in 1960, during one of the famous televised debates between presidential candidates Richard Nixon and John F. Kennedy, Nixon demanded that Kennedy renounce the earthy language favoured by his supporter ex-President Harry Truman, and cited Eisenhower, his Republican predecessor, as a champion of 'the dignity of the office'. In response, Kennedy laughed.

After the event had ended, Nixon was asked by reporters how he thought the whole debate went. 'That fucking bastard!' he replied. 'He wasn't supposed to be using notes!'

Dick Cheney

The US Vice President shocked the Senate with his unparliamentary language in June 2004. While the members of the Senate were having their annual group photograph taken, Democrat Pat Leahy and Republican Dick Cheney came to verbal blows, purportedly over Leahy's recent accusations of Cheney's involvement in some dodgy business contracts in Iraq.

The 'debate' ended with Cheney urging Leahy to 'go fuck' himself. 'I think he was just having a bad day,' Leahy said afterwards. 'I was kind of shocked to hear that kind of language on the floor.'

Winston Churchill

Wartime Prime Minister Sir Winston Churchill was well known as a wit and raconteur, with a sharp retort to any quip or criticism always to hand. However, it was in the role of Home Secretary, an office which he took in 1910, in which he upheld the standard for profanity lovers everywhere. Determined to reform the prison service, he decided to start by ensuring that 'next year there will be 50,000 fewer people sent to prison than last year.' At that time, 5,000 boys between the ages of sixteen and twenty-one were sent to prison for minor offences, including swearing, and Churchill proposed that disciplinary exercise rather than a prison sentence should be the punishment.

Winston himself could utter the odd blasphemy, as he did when he met the prime minister of Pakistan who, as a devout Muslim, never touched the sauce. The occasion was a formal dinner at Buckingham Palace. Winston's question: 'Will you have a whisky and soda, Mr Prime Minister?' was followed by this exchange.

'No, thank you!'
'What's that?'
'No, thank you!'
'What? Why?'
'I'm a teetotaller, Mr Prime Minister.'
'What's that?'
'I'm a teetotaller!'
'A teetotaller? Christ! I mean God! I mean Allah!'

On another occasion Churchill was in a House of Commons toilet when Clement Attlee entered, prompting Churchill to turn his back on his colleague. Attlee asked, 'Feeling stand-offish today, are we, Winston?' Churchill replied, 'That's right. Every time you see something big, you want to nationalize it.'

Derivation: 'Twat'

    a) noun – female genitalia
    b) noun – an idiot

Although this has the same literal meaning as 'cunt', it is considered less offensive as a term of abuse and is usually also taken to mean 'fool' or 'idiot' when directed at another person. In fact, many of those who use it in this way may not know of its original meaning, for 'twat' comes from an Old Norse word meaning 'cut' or 'slit'.

Other words that have come to refer to the same part of the female anatomy include 'pussy', 'muff', 'minge' and, in Scotland, 'fud'.

Variations include: twot, twatted, twat-faced

John Major

Once known as the grey man of politics, John Major probably went up in everybody's estimation when, in 1993, his frustration with right-wing Tories led him to refer to them as 'bastards'. The attack against the Eurosceptics in his party was inadvertently taped after an interview at Downing Street with ITN's political editor Michael Brunson, while the technicians left the line open to record 'cutaways' (the silent shots used to cover gaps in an edited interview).

Mr Brunson mentioned three rebel cabinet ministers who had threatened to resign over Mr Major's stance on the Maastricht

Treaty, and asked why they weren't sacked.

The Prime Minister answered: 'I could bring in other people. But where do you think most of this poison is coming from? From the dispossessed and the never-possessed. You can think of ex-ministers who are going around causing all sorts of trouble. We don't want another three more of the bastards out there.'

Michael Mates

Sadly for him, the Rt Hon. Michael Mates MP is better remembered for a phrase than a political career as far as the general public are concerned.

A Conservative MP since 1974, he began to enjoy a ministerial career in the early 1990s but, unfortunately, this wasn't to last. While serving as Minister of State in the Northern Ireland office it emerged that he had a close relationship with businessman Asil Nadir, who fled to Cyprus as a fugitive when his business, Polly Peck, collapsed under suspicions of fraud, embezzlement and false accounting.

The evidence brought to light a watch that Mates had given Mr Nadir, which he'd had inscribed with 'Don't let the buggers get you down'. Mates resigned from his post at the Northern Ireland office in June 1993.

Bleeping Broadcasting

In 1987 Colin Morris, then Director of Religious Education at the BBC, said: 'The broadcaster is a guest in the home of the viewer and there are things which guests can be expected not to do while enjoying their guests' hospitality ... when broadcasters introduce offensive language or images into the family setting, they are guilty of a double offence: they have forced into the consciousness issues that may be embarrassing across the generations, and as guests in the home they have breached the laws of hospitality.'

Despite this eloquent entreaty, television has not always been the most courteous of guests in our homes and, on one or two occasions, has displayed the sort of behaviour that would normally ensure that guest was never invited back.

The first memorable event in the story of small-screen profanity occurred in 1965. Flamboyant theatre critic Kenneth Tynan made television history when he used the word 'fuck' during a BBC broadcast. Tynan, a hugely accomplished and often controversial journalist, was taking part in a live debate on, appropriately enough, censorship, and expressed his views thus: 'I doubt if there are any rational people to whom the word "fuck" would be particularly diabolical, revolting or totally forbidden.'

The events that followed seem to have proved the statement somewhat wrong. The BBC produced an official apology, 133 MPs signed four separate motions in the House of Commons, and campaigner Mary Whitehouse wrote a letter to the Queen suggesting that Tynan 'ought to have his bottom spanked'. (Something that he probably would have enjoyed given his love of sadomasochism that was later to come to light.) Mary Whitehouse's campaign against the moral laxity of the BBC was strengthened by the incident – and Tynan's television career was over.

Another journalist, Peregrine Worsthorne, almost brought about his own downfall by saying 'fuck' on TV some eight years later. When Conservative minister Lord Lambton was found in bed with a call girl, Worsthorne was asked what he thought the public reaction was likely to be. *The Daily Telegraph* columnist replied that they 'will not give a fuck'. As he recalled in a recent interview, 'next morning my television gaffe was on the front page of all the morning newspapers – except *The Daily Telegraph* – and I was suspended from broadcasting by the newspaper for some months.'

The BBC was inundated with complaints and issued an apology, then promptly cancelled the programmes that Worsthorne had been scheduled to make. Following the faux pas, again the issue was raised in Parliament and the journalist was temporarily demoted from his position as the Deputy Editor of *The Daily Telegraph*.

●

In 1976, punk bad-boys the Sex Pistols caused outrage when a live interview, conducted by the starchy Bill Grundy, degenerated into a string of obscenities. After being asked about the money they had received for their record contract, guitarist Steve Jones told him, 'We've fuckin' spent it.' Johnny Rotten then used the words 'tough shit' before Grundy, increasingly annoyed, challenged the lads to say something 'outrageous'; Jones, as you can see in the transcript below, accepted the challenge.

> *Grundy: Well, keep going, chief, keep going. Go on, you've got another five seconds. Say something outrageous.*
> *Jones: You dirty bastard!*
> *Grundy: Go on, again.*
> *Jones: You dirty fucker! [Laughter from the group]*
> *Grundy: What a clever boy!*
> *Jones: What a fucking rotter.*

The following day the newspapers were full of headlines like 'The Filth and the Fury', the public were shocked and the group was banned from TV. Bill Grundy was suspended from work for two weeks, and shortly afterwards the programme, *Today*, was taken off the air. These days the event probably wouldn't make a line in the gossip columns! In fact, in 2004, when the same Johnny Rotten (now going by his real name, John Lydon) called the voting public 'fucking cunts' on *I'm a Celebrity, Get Me Out of Here*, there were fewer than 100 complaints.

●

The first use of the word 'cunt' on British TV was in *Mosley*, a four-part series about the rise and fall of the British fascist leader Sir Oswald Mosley, which was screened in 1998. Surprisingly, the Independent Television Commission (the ITC, the predecessor to Ofcom, which regulates TV and radio transmissions) only received seven complaints and refused to uphold them, saying:

> *At this late stage in the drama, the full extent of Mosley's fascist beliefs had been exposed. The prison warder's language expressed the anger he felt towards Mosley. Seen against this background, the ITC did not believe that the use of the language was gratuitous. The ITC also took into account the fact that the scene occurred at 10 p.m., well after the 9 p.m. watershed, and that viewers had been made aware that the episode contained bad language by an announcement at the start.*

TFI Friday

This anarchic chat show presented and produced by Chris Evans, the maverick DJ and television presenter who came to prominence in the nineties, was always intended to be controversial. But Chris got more than he bargained for when the Happy Mondays' front man Shaun Ryder made an appearance.

As a result of bad language in a previous show, Chris Evans had asked Shaun not to swear during the interview. So he didn't.

However, when Ryder took to the stage to perform a cover version of the Sex Pistols' hit 'Pretty Vacant', he had slightly changed the lyrics – by adding thirteen 'Fucks'! At this time the show was broadcast live so there was no opportunity to bleep over the words. The ITC condemned the broadcast as a 'serious breach' of the programme code, and the show was made to change to a pre-recorded format to prevent further such incidents from occurring.

On another occasion the programme got into hot water over an interview between Chris Evans and American 'shock jock' DJ Howard Stern, which contained 'crude remarks and sexual innuendo'. Even worse, a seven-year-old girl became so upset after she failed to win a £15,000 speedboat for her family that the ITC accused the show of 'emotional abuse'. *TFI Friday* was axed by Channel Four in 2000.

Incidentally the title, a play on the phrase 'Thank God it's Friday' is controversial in itself. The official line was that the 'F' stood for 'Four' (as in Channel Four) and that any variation on what the 'F' stood for was entirely in the viewers' imagination!

The Osbournes

When rocker Ozzy Osbourne and his wife Sharon agreed to let the cameras into their home for a weekly series, a cult show was born. The show, which featured the daily life of the couple, two children (Kelly and Jack), and numerous pets, quickly became the most popular show on MTV and was brought to British TV by Channel Four.

Much of the time the show was filled with bitching, fighting and a great deal of swearing. Episode one, 'There Goes the Neighbourhood', saw the family moving into their Beverly Hills mansion with their menagerie of pets. It had a swear count of fifty-six. The second episode, featuring their dog shitting all over the house, raised the swear count to eighty-six, and not one of the shows in each of the three series went out with less than thirty swear words.

By the time the final show was broadcast, viewing figures had hit the eight million mark, and MTV was showing a pre-watershed version called *The Bleeping Osbournes,* in which all swear words were replaced with bleeps and farmyard noises. Kelly and Jack had become famous in their own right and Sharon had become a judge on *The X Factor*, on which she managed not to swear, despite several spats with fellow judge Simon Cowell.

The family also earned a shitload of money – reported to be around $85m (£46m) as sales of 'Ozzy' merchandise rose to $50m (£27.2m), a record for a heavy-metal musician. Ozzy himself wondered why it was so popular, reasoning, 'I suppose Americans get a kick out of watching a crazy Brit family like us make complete fools of ourselves every week.'

Bizarrely, in spite of an episode in which Kelly broke down to a family therapist and claimed her childhood lacked a father, Ozzy and Sharon were voted the UK's most popular parents in a 2005 poll, beating Charles and Camilla, Posh and Becks, Richard and Judy and the Blairs by winning 43 per cent of the vote. This must have come as some surprise to Sharon, who once said that when it came to parenting, she 'had seriously fucked up'.

In 2004 Sharon and Ozzy recorded an advert for Children in Need in which Sharon promised the British public that her husband would stop swearing for twenty-four hours to raise money for the charity. The advert showed Ozzy with his mouth taped shut but, halfway through, the ageing rocker rips off his tape and shouts, 'No swear fucking words? You've got to be fucking joking! I'm the Prince of Darkness – they expect me to fucking swear!'

During an interview, Ozzy was asked whether he had any advice for the young bands performing at the Ozzfest concert. He mulled the question briefly before giving his measured response: 'Fuck off.' On another occasion he met TV host Carson Daly at MTV. Daly congratulated the self-proclaimed 'Prince of Fucking Darkness' on the success of his show.

'Fucking Ozzy, man,' he praised. 'I fucking love the show, it fucking rocks, you fucking rule. It's a fucking killer!'

After Daly left, Ozzy remarked, 'Nice enough guy, but his language was atrocious.'

Deadwood

David Milch's Wild West serial *Deadwood* was nominated for eleven Emmys in its first season, but attracted as much controversy as praise. With seventy-three swear words packed into its first hour-long episode, the drama, first screened in the UK in September 2004, contained more profanities than any other serial in history.

Set in the town of Deadwood, South Dakota, in the 1870s, the show portrays the brutal way of life of the settlement at the height of the gold rush, when the murder rate was one a day. Starring British actor Ian McShane as the aptly named Al Swearengen, the thirteen-week series contained 831 uses of the F-word, and the dialogue was punctuated with so many expletives that US reviewers complained of being unable to follow the plot. Several Internet sites were even set up to tot up the number of profanities in each episode.

The first episode alone contained the following swear count:

'fuck' – 49	*'cunt'* – 3
'cocksucker' – 8	*'pissing'* – 2
'shit' – 7	*'motherfucker'* – 1
'son of a bitch' – 1	*'sweet-assed'* – 1

and one lowly 'bastard'

Although there were many complaints about the foul language in the show, writer David Milch, a former professor of English at Yale University, says he conducted extensive research into the dialect of the pioneers and he feels that he got it right. As he told one newspaper, 'There have been a great many people complaining that this is not the way people spoke in the Wild West, but what they are really saying is that this is not the way people spoke in John Ford movies.

'Bad language is a form of armour, a way to assert strength and masculinity. Any society that is poor or lawless or violent uses profanity as a way of protection. Go to any inner-city ghetto from Los Angeles to Glasgow and you will find an excess of foul-mouthed men. To pretend that this was not the case in Deadwood, the most lawless and violent outpost of a lawless and violent country, is patently absurd.'

However, the author of the novel that spawned the series, Peter Dexter, disagrees. In a separate interview he commented, 'In my view, it is not correctly representing how things were in Deadwood in the 1870s.

'The producers are just using the excessive language to sensationalize the show. I'm not saying the language wouldn't have been used at all. But people in Deadwood preferred to shoot off their guns rather than their mouths.'

Jerry Springer – The Opera

After an incredibly successful run in London's West End, *Jerry Springer – The Opera* was screened by the BBC in January 2005. The musical, already famous for its perceived blasphemy and high swear count, portrays a struggle between Jesus and the Devil for the soul of the infamous chat-show host and, at one point, has the two participate in a swearing contest. The decision to screen the musical caused instant controversy – the BBC received 45,000 complaints *before* the day of transmission. As the show aired, 800 protesters rallied outside the Corporation's headquarters. One journalist estimated the on-air profanity count at 8,283, which included 3,168 'fucks' and 297 'cunts'. To reach this astonishing figure, however, every swear word uttered by the twenty-seven-performer-strong chorus was counted individually.

Stewart Lee, one of the writers of the show, defended the swear count in an article printed in *The Daily Telegraph*:

A pressure group called Mediawatch is orchestrating a campaign against the show, which it maintains includes 8,000 swear words, 3,168 of them 'fucks' and 297 of them 'cunts'. There are actually seven 'cunts' in the show – four of them adjectives, and three of them nouns. At the National Theatre, the sentence in which they all appear often received a standing ovation.

There are, in fact, 117 'fucks' in the show, all of them sung beautifully by a hugely talented cast, leaving Mediawatch with a shortfall of 3,051 'fucks'. *The Daily Telegraph* has gone to the trouble of counting all the swear words in the show and pegs the figure at 451, some 7,549 less than Mediawatch's figure, but I think the organization must have included category B and C obscenities such as 'ass', 'poop' and 'nipple' to hit this score. Perhaps Mediawatch multiplied the swear words by the number of people singing on stage. Who knows? Whatever, this means Channel Four's screening of Tarantino's *Reservoir Dogs* is still the most profane thing ever seen on British TV, which at least leaves something to aim for.

The Mary Whitehouse Experience

The joy of swearing has not always been a pleasure endorsed by the media or, indeed, those in it.

Mary Whitehouse was a schoolmistress from the Midlands who became the voice of the 'moral majority' in the sixties and seventies. She first became concerned about the effect of TV's sexual content on her pupils, but she broadened her fight to include opposition both to violence and bad language.

Initially, the BBC's Director General Sir Hugh Greene ignored pleas to halt the slide of liberalism on the BBC, but then invoked a huge swell of criticism with his screening of the play *Up the Junction* in 1965, which contained an abortion scene and plenty of bad language. In the same year (also the year that Kenneth Tynan uttered British TV's first 'fuck'), Mary Whitehouse set up the National Viewers' and Listeners' Association, which is now known as Mediawatch. The Government began to take notice of such pressure groups and drafted in Lord Hill of Luton, the head of the Independent Television Authority (ITA), to become the chairman of the BBC Board of Governors in order to 'sort out' the BBC. The regulation of the commercial stations remained the remit of the ITA, later named the Independent Broadcasting Association (IBA) and then the Independent Television Commission (ITC). More recently the various television watchdogs have been merged to become Ofcom.

Derivation: 'Cunt'

a) noun – female genitalia
b) noun – stupid or nasty person

The C-word, as it is often known, remains the most taboo word in the English language, despite its increasing use in film and on television. It is also one of the oldest words in the swearing vocabulary, hailing from around AD 1230.

The origin of the word is Germanic, from the Old Norse *kunta*, Middle Dutch *kunte* and possibly High German 'kotze', meaning 'prostitute'. Also perhaps of relevance is the Latin, *kuntus* – 'wedge'. The word appears in Chaucer's *The Canterbury Tales* as 'queynte' but, in Middle English, was often spelt 'counte'.

As a word that has long been most offensive to women, it has also galvanized feminists into action in the past. In 2000, women in Penn State in the US held a 'Cuntfest' with the intention of reclaiming the word!

Variations include: cunt-struck, cunting

The Birth of the 'Melon Farmer'

When British director Alex Cox was asked to tone down his 1984 film *Repo Man*, starring Emilio Estevez and Harry Dean Stanton, so that it could be shown on TV, he decided that blanking or bleeping the prolific use of bad language would spoil the film. He came up with an ingenious alternative. Every 'fuck' and 'fuckin'' became 'flip' and 'flippin'' and, most famously, he overdubbed 'motherfucker' with 'melon farmer'.

By proving that censorship can be achieved with a certain amount of wit, he delivered a film with such immortal lines as 'Flip you, melon farmer!' The 1977 film *Slap Shot*, starring Paul Newman, was peppered with the F-word but, when it was shown on TV, it became the first film to be dubbed with the word 'freakin''. In the US, the replacement word soon took on a life of its own and is now frequently used in everyday speech.

Another film that got the film-to-TV treatment was the 1979 Steve Martin comedy *The Jerk*. 'Suck my toes!' was apparently too risqué for its sensitive, early eighties audience, and had to be changed to 'scratch my toes!'

Other Films Which Suffered From 'Melon Farmer' Syndrome

The Usual Suspects – 'Hand me the keys, you fucking cocksucker' was changed to 'Hand me the keys, you fairy godmother' for the TV screening.

The Silence of Lambs – The line 'I can smell your cunt' was also filmed with the C-word substituted by 'scent', and this was the version shown on TV.

Die Hard – the TV edit removes the word 'motherfucker', so we hear Bruce Willis saying, in his most menacing voice, 'Yippee-ki-yay, *Mr Falcon*'.

Robocop – 'Don't frig with me, mothercrusher.' No explanation needed.

Monty Python's Censored Circus

From 1969 to 1974, six lads from Cambridge University sent shockwaves through the BBC with their anarchic sense of humour. John Cleese, Graham Chapman, Eric Idle, Michael Palin, Terry Gilliam and Terry Jones were young, wild and wacky, and inevitably the scripts to their show, *Monty Python's Flying Circus,* often contained the sort of words that were unlikely to get past the straight-laced execs of the BBC. No surprise, then, that by the time the show hit the screen the rude words had often been substituted for 'something completely different'.

The sketch 'Proust' is one of the most famous pieces of self-censorship. Asked by quizmaster Terry Jones what his hobbies are, Graham Chapman's contestant answers 'golf, strangling animals and masturbating'. This original version was recorded but, when it came to its first broadcast in November 1972, the words 'and masturbating' were removed, leaving a second of silence. The TV audience heard a massive laugh from the studio audience and wondered what was so funny. However, for the 1979 repeat, the line was left intact, and it has since appeared uncensored on the 1987 repeat, and on both the 1986 BBC video and its BMG re-release.

In another sketch the word 'tit' was removed, so that a comment on Clive Jenkins being 'blue in the tits' became 'blue in the breasts', while the phrase, 'Will you shut your gob, you tit?' was also toned down.

In the legendary 'Cheese Sketch' the script reads, 'I don't care how bleep runny it is', which suggests that that they were originally going to include the word 'fucking' and bleep it out. This later became 'excrementally runny'.

Live 8

The screening of the 2005 Live 8 concert was a triumph for the BBC and attracted an audience of 9.6 million viewers. However, it was not without its problems. As it was live, and much of what was shown was pre-watershed with many children watching, it was a case of *who* would swear, rather than *if*. In fact it was Madonna and, surprise, surprise, Snoop Dogg who were the worst offenders, and their acts attracted 400 complaints to the BBC.

The biggest shock of all was that the famously foul-mouthed Sir Bob Geldof managed to keep it clean throughout the whole day. The only people not so chuffed about it were the bookies. Bookmakers William Hill had taken a string of bets that Sir Bob would not utter a single swear word during the entire concert; in fact, they received so many bets that they slashed the odds from 20/1 to 8/1. 'It will be us using the bad language if he causes us to make a five-figure payout as a result,' a Hill spokesman said.

You Can't Say 'Tits' on the Radio
(With apologies to the Scissor Sisters)

It is not unheard of for the occasional swear word to escape over the radio waves, but the use of more severe profanity is yet to become as commonplace as it is on TV and film – though its perpetrators are not beyond getting their knuckles rapped. Complaints made to the regulating body (as of 2003 this is Ofcom, which brought together The Radio Authority, Broadcasting Standards Commission, the ITC, Oftel, the Radio Authority and the Radiocommunications Agency) are considered with a number of factors in mind, including context. The Broadcasting Code, Section 2 – 'Harm and Offence' states that 'applying generally accepted standards broadcasters must ensure that material which may cause offence is justified by the context [. . .] Such material may include, but is not limited to, offensive language . . . [and] discriminatory treatment or language.' And although there is no official watershed when it comes to radio broadcasting (unlike the 9 p.m. observance for television), if there's a chance minors may be listening the authority is very clear about what is acceptable, stating:

Offensive language must not be broadcast before the watershed, or when children are particularly likely to be listening, unless it is justified by the context. In any event, frequent use of such language must be avoided before the watershed.

Despite such stringent regulations, it's fortunate then that for connoisseurs of cursing the airwaves haven't always been squeaky clean. The early days of radio were relatively restrained – though Max Miller and the *Round the Horne* team were exceptions. However, the rise of so-called 'Shock Jocks' in the US and the 'lads' and 'ladettes' of the DJ world in the UK has led, inevitably, to more instances of profanity – both deliberate and accidental – and the fact that radio is usually broadcast live leaves little opportunity for bleeps, and plenty for complaints!

Round the Horne

From 1965 to 1969 the nation gathered around its radios on Sunday afternoons for an anarchic mixture of wit and innuendo delivered by a hugely talented bunch of comedians. Barry Took and Marty Feldman wrote the show, which starred Kenneth Horne, Kenneth Williams, Betty Marsden, Bill Pertwee, Douglas Smith and Hugh Paddick.

The show, which at its peak attracted 15 million listeners, had such memorable characters as J. Peasemold Gruntfuttock (a dirty old man), Daphne Whitethigh (a parody of Fanny Cradock) and Dame Celia Molestrangler.

The saucy nature of the language offended some. Sir Cyril Black and Mary Whitehouse objected to the blasphemy of one particular sketch featuring J. Peasemold Gruntfuttock. Although they succeeded in getting the script changed, the then BBC Director General, Hugh Greene, stood by the risqué content of the show as a whole, and refused to bow to pressure or ask the writers and actors to 'tone it down'.

The use of swear words would then still have been anathema on the radio, although they may have been in more general use in the street in the post-war years. The *Round the Horne* writers got over this comedic hurdle by using wordplay and innuendo, making up nonsense words that sounded vaguely rude but which would get past the censors.

Rambling Syd Rumpo, a singing yokel played by the inimitable Kenneth Williams, sang songs to familiar tunes but with new (and mangled) lyrics. 'Nadgers', 'cordwangle' and 'wogglers' were just some of the words that appeared in his songs, some extracts of which are below.

'The Taddle Groper's Dance'
(To the tune of 'Here We Go Round the Mulberry Bush')

There's cordwangles in my possett bag
What shall I do Mary O –
And I can't woggle my artefacts
What shall I do my Darling

. . . .

But now I've nadgered my artefacts
What shall I do my darling?

Rambling Syd: 'So she tells him what to do with his artefacts and he does it – and they dance off woggling and groping their taddles.'

45

'The Australian Outlaw's Song'
(To the tune of 'Waltzing Matilda')

Once long ago in the shade of a goolie bush
Toasting his splod by the faggots gleam
Rested a gander man nobbling with his woggle iron
And stuffing a sheep in the Old Mill Stream.
Then up came the troupers and hung him by
  the billabong
They twisted his woggle irons one two three
Now his ghost sits and moans
As it grunges in his gander can
Who'll come a woggling his jumbuck with me.

Seven Dirty Words

In 1975, US comedian George Carlin landed himself in hot water when he recorded a monologue entitled 'Filthy Words', which was then played on Pacifica Radio Station WBAI-FM. The sketch revolved around the seven words that you are not allowed to say on radio, being 'shit', 'piss', 'fuck', 'cunt', 'cocksucker', 'motherfucker' and 'tits'.

Furious that his son had heard the broadcast a listener complained to the Federal Communications Commission (FCC), who asked the radio station for a response, issuing a warning to WBAI that 'in the event subsequent complaints are received, the Commission will then decide whether it should utilize any of the available sanctions it has been granted by Congress.'

Pacifica took the case to the Court of Appeals and won. The FCC took Pacifica to the Supreme Court and won, and this decision formally established the indecency regulations in American broadcasting. In follow-up rulings, the FCC clarified that the words might be acceptable under certain circumstances, particularly at times when children would not be expected to be listening. Today, 'tits' and 'piss' are generally no longer prohibited from broadcast over public airwaves.

Howard Stern

Howard Stern started his career as a DJ at an obscure New York radio station, but his foul mouth and constant talk about sex led to a huge following and, in 1990, his show went US-wide. The 'Shock Jock' had arrived.

Fame spread fast, and so did controversy. Never afraid to offend, his crude style led to constant fines and condemnation, as well as admiration from legions of fans. On one show, for example, he brought a female listener to orgasm over the telephone by making deep buzzing noises into his microphone while she sat on a speaker with the volume turned up. On another occasion he was fined for a graphic conversation about anal sex.

Stern was sacked from six stations after regulators fined Clear Channel Communications $495,000 (£280,000) for a show which featured Rick Salomon, whose only claim to fame is the release of a video showing him having sex with Paris Hilton. Clear Channel eventually decided, in 2004, to cut their losses and part with Stern after receiving a $500,000 (£284,000) fine from the FCC.

Howard Stern was the pioneer of the 'Shock Jock' phenomenon and many followed in his footsteps. Many, too, have since been sacked in the backlash against the ever more offensive broadcasts.

In a 'zero tolerance' blitz, Clear Channel fired Stern's colleague Bubba the Love Sponge after a sexual stunt and, the day after Stern's departure, Larry Wachs and Eric Von Haessler were fired from Atlanta's WKLS-FM, owned by the same company. The two DJs, known as 'The Regular Guys', got their marching orders after listeners heard a conversation of a sexual nature when they left a microphone on during a break. The presenters said it was accidental.

DJs Opie and Anthony had their nationally syndicated 'extreme talk' show cancelled after they aired a running commentary of a couple having sex at a New York cathedral. For years they had been getting away with their own brand of swearing, by using just initials. 'You know, I'd F you in the A right now,' Anthony once remarked to an attractive guest. 'I'd take my D, rub it all over your T's and blow my S all over your F! Open up, you wily bitch!'

Loud-mouthed DJs

British DJs are also capable of shooting their mouths and arousing the ire of the authorities, and a survey in 2000 identified that the main reason for the increase in the number of obscene incidents was the stations' desperate attempts to win listeners – particularly on programmes broadcast at key times such as the breakfast or 'drivetime' shows.

The research, commissioned by the Broadcasting Standards Commission, showed that of the parents asked, 56 per cent worried that their children would be exposed to offensive material on the radio and 85 per cent said daytime swearing should be banned. Nearly 15 per cent of respondents said they disliked rudeness towards phone-in callers, while 14 per cent cited bad language as a cause for concern, 7 per cent disapproved of sexual innuendo and 7 per cent criticized 'explicit or controversial' song lyrics.

Some examples of radio rudeness: in November 1998, former Radio One DJ Zoë Ball was disciplined after using the F-word while talking about a concert of her husband, Fatboy Slim; in December 1999, XFM was fined £50,000 for broadcasting two breakfast shows that included material offensive language and comments about bestiality; Radio Two DJs Mark and Lard came under fire in 2003 when Ofcom criticized an edition of their show in which Mark Radcliffe swore while in conversation with his co-host. As the show was in the early afternoon the use of bad language, although accidental, was condemned as 'ill-judged'.

Oops! I Did it Again

Radio Five Live presenter Nicky Campbell made a Freudian slip in the extended debate about fox hunting – not once, but twice.

The popular breakfast host stumbled over his words as he

interviewed a huntswoman and tried to say 'West Kent Hunt'. He introduced her with the words: 'Georgie Wordsley is master of the Old Surrey and Burstow and West cunt . . . er, hunt!'

'I do apologize for that,' he offered immediately. 'It's very early in the morning. I am extremely embarrassed about it.' Lo and behold, a few weeks later, he was doing a show about the sorts of news events that would still be remembered in 500 years. 'Lots of you are mentioning that you will still be talking about the cunt,' he said.

After a short, shocked silence he stuttered, 'Err, that's the West Kent Hunt.'

He then added, 'I don't believe it. I do not believe it.'

A BBC spokeswoman later said, 'He was trying to read a text message from a listener when he made an unfortunate and unintentional slip of the tongue.

'He is very embarrassed to have been caught out by this seemingly innocent phrase again.'

More Blue Bloopers

In March 2003, Granada news presenter (and founder of Factory Records) Tony Wilson created a stir when, during an afternoon news bulletin, he shouted at some production staff. He had no idea his outburst was going out live. 'None of the fucking lights are working, guys!' he was heard to shout. 'Camera one you have no red fucking light on . . . '

The switchboard lit up soon enough. Granada was forced to apologize 'unreservedly for any offence caused to viewers. We would like to stress the incident was entirely unintentional and Anthony was not aware his remarks were being broadcast.'

Derivation: 'Bollocks'

a) noun – testicles
b) noun – rubbish
c) interjection – expression of annoyance

One of the most satisfying exclamations in the language, 'bollocks' can be used as term for testicles, but is more often used to mean 'rubbish' ('you're talking bollocks') or as a general expletive ('Oh, bollocks!').

To 'give a bollocking' is to tear someone off a strip. This is often changed to 'rollocking'.

It is also used in the phrase 'the dog's bollocks', which refers to something that is excellent, the best of its kind and is often adapted to 'the mutt's nuts'. 'The dog's bollocks' derives, according to one story, from the wording on the packaging of 1950s children's construction kits, such as Meccano, which came in boxes of various sizes. The standard-sized box had the words 'Box, Standard' on the front, which became 'bog standard'. The largest box was the 'Box, Deluxe', which, you've guessed it, was spoonerized to become 'the dog's bollocks'.

The origin of the word 'bollocks' is a matter of dispute. The most likely, however, is that it comes from the Germanic *ballock*, which itself came from the Old English *bealluc*, which referred to a ball or spherical object. Other words used to refer to the testicles are 'balls', 'knackers', 'nuts', 'cobblers' and 'rocks'.

Variations include: bollix, bollocking, stark-bollock naked, bollixed (drunk)

In 2004, CNN were covering John Kerry's acceptance speech at the Democratic Convention when a barrage of expletives was heard on air. Technician Don Mischer was overheard complaining that balloons in the hall were not being released quickly enough. 'Go, balloons. Go, balloons. Go, balloons,' he shouted. 'Come on, guys! Let's move it. Jesus. We need more balloons . . . Go, confetti. Go, confetti. Go, confetti. I want more balloons . . . Why the hell is nothing falling? What the fuck are you guys doing up there? More balloons, more balloons!'

●

Alan Hansen and Ian Wright were understandably upset when England lost to Brazil in the 2002 World Cup. While they vented their feelings, however, someone forgot to turn off their microphones. Digital viewers saw their screens go blank, but could still hear the panel discussing the game. 'Seaman was fucking five yards off his line!' fumed Wright. 'And what the fuck was he [manager Sven-Göran Eriksson] doing taking Michael Owen off?'

To add insult to injury, when asked which match was coming up next, Hansen replied, 'It's the fucking Krauts!'

The BBC later apologized, blaming a technical fault. 'Obviously Gary [Lineker], Alan, Peter [Reid] and Ian were unaware they were on air. It was a private conversation between friends and no offence was intended.'

Famous Foul-mouths: Song Sung Blue

The punks and rappers of the world may take delight in profane lyrics, but most artists try to keep the record clean. However, it could be said that when many of them stop singing, that's when the swearing starts; away from the recording studios, even the most revered artists have less than lyrical language.

Sir Elton John

Outspoken DJ Chris Moyles was almost speechless when the elder statesman of pop turned the airwaves blue during a Radio One breakfast interview. Sir Elton had been warned beforehand not to swear, but was unaware the show was going out live. Declaring he hadn't been to the BBC for so long that he'd almost gone to their old building, he said, 'I saw Tony Blackburn with a walking stick and thought "wrong fucking place".'

Realizing what he'd said, he asked, 'I'm not live on air, am I?'

'Yes, we're live,' Moyles told the singer. 'I apologize to the young boys and girls. But it is Elton John.'

Sir Elton went on to describe his Las Vegas show as having 'more tits than anything else' before adding, 'You can't say "tits" on the radio, according to the Scissor Sisters.'

Unabashed, Elton continued. Could he say 'wank'? 'Vagina'? 'Testicles'? Finally, referring to a previous guest on the show, he asked, 'Did Gwen Stefani swear? No? Bollocks.' At the end, he promised to come back the following week if he could say 'bugger'.

Chris Moyles immediately apologized again, before saying 'Thanks everyone, you're listening to my last show on Radio One.' A Radio One spokeswoman later apologized.

Sir Elton, who was seen swearing profusely in the documentary *Tantrums and Tiaras,* is notorious for such outbursts and once berated Madonna at an award ceremony hosted by *Q* magazine. Accepting his prize he called Jonathan Ross a 'ponce' before saying 'Madonna! Best fucking live act! Fuck off!' and accusing her of lip syncing. 'That's me off her fucking Christmas card list, but do I give a toss?'

The flamboyant star also commissioned a £7,000 ring encrusted with diamonds which spelled out a message. 'It's very funny,' he declared. The message? 'Fuck you.'

Bob Geldof

In 1985, Bob Geldof and Midge Ure organized the biggest pop-music event in history. Live Aid immortalized in the memory visions of teeming crowds, global transmission, the greatest performers of the age and, of course, the millions of pounds raised for the starving population of Africa. Ask anyone over the age of thirty what they remember about the concert and their recollections of the musical highlights will vary. The one thing everybody is clear on is the moment that Bob Geldof grabbed the mike and shouted, 'Just give us your fucking money!'

The Irish singer and former frontman of The Boomtown Rats probably holds the record for the most watched incident of swearing on TV, as the attention-grabbing phrase was heard by 30 million people in the UK alone, and was screened around the world. Mind you, it did the trick. Live Aid raised a total of £150 million.

Just to prove that turning fifty and getting a knighthood hasn't mellowed the old punk, Bob is still prone to the odd outburst.

When launching Live 8 in 2005, two decades after the original event, Bob held a press conference to which Bono, a keen supporter of the cause, was intending to contribute via satellite link. By the time Geldof was ready to talk to the U2 singer they had overrun their allotted satellite time. 'Are you there, Bono?' said Geldof. 'Ah, well, fuck off then. We know what you were going to say anyway.'

Bob even managed to utter the F-word during a kids' show. In 2003 he appeared on live Saturday-morning show *CD:UK* and was annoyed that a video clip of No Doubt's *It's My Life* couldn't be played because it would overrun the scheduled showing of another clip. 'Do it anyway. Fuck the tape,' he said. Presenter Cat Deeley replied, 'We can't use that kind of language at this time in the morning,' before telling Bob, 'You were doing so well there as well!'

Still, somehow the word 'fuck' sounds so much better with an Irish accent!

Madonna

Michigan's own material girl is not exactly 'like a virgin' when it comes to her potty mouth. She is notorious for swearing during her shows and, in 2001, she was asked to announce the winner of the Turner Prize at the Tate Modern in London. 'At a time when political correctness is valued over honesty,' she began, 'I would also like to say . . . Right on, motherfucker! Everyone is a winner!' An incisive observation on the state of modern art, certainly.

When Warner Bros launched Madonna's 2003 album *American Life,* they released fake versions of the title track into the public domain, aimed at those who download free music illegally. Instead of the track, the file contained a sound-clip of Madonna saying, 'What the fuck do you think you are doing?' Unfortunately, the tactic backfired somewhat. Firstly, the message became a cult hit in its own right when the sample was remixed into other compositions. Even worse, an enterprising hacker replaced her website with a near-blank page that stated 'This is what the fuck I think I'm doing', and offered download links to the actual song. Warner Bros pulled the website offline and it remained inaccessible for fifteen hours while their techies attempted to undo the damage.

Bizarrely, for one who is so fond of a fulsome oath, Madonna imposed a cursing fine during her 2004 Reinvention tour. 'She has paid plenty [herself],' publicist Liz Rosenberg admitted. 'I think it is $5 a curse word.' According to *The New York Post*, her dancers caught the sharp end of her tongue if they didn't get their moves right. She was heard to scream at the hapless hoofers, 'Get it right or get the fuck out!' And, continuing Bob Geldof's tradition, viewers were astounded to hear Madonna's greeting to the crowd at Live 8 – 'Are you fucking ready London?' Let's hope Lourdes and Rocco weren't watching . . .

Literary Language

Good authors too, who once knew
better words
Now only know four-letter words
Writing prose
Anything goes.
COLE PORTER, 'ANYTHING GOES' (1934)

Writers throughout history have peppered their books and plays with the choicest phrases – phrases to shock, to seduce, to teach or to preach. Attitudes to invective language in books and plays has changed throughout the centuries and what shocked the audience of an English theatre in 1914 would seem tame in a modern-day production.

For example, the publication of a novel entitled *Cunt* (by Stewart Home) in 1999 barely raised an eyebrow, yet J. D. Salinger's cult novel *Catcher in the Rye* caused outrage in the 1950s because of its frequent use of the words 'goddamn' and 'damn'.

Some authors, such as Shakespeare and Chaucer, hid many of their profanities with clever puns, while others, such as D. H. Lawrence and Philip Larkin, were happy to 'publish and be damned'. Below is a select look at swearing in literature.

Geoffrey 'cheeky' Chaucer

Anybody who studied Chaucer's *The Canterbury Tales* at school will no doubt remember the sniggers behind the desktops as the archaic language was finally translated, in many cases, to reveal something of a bawdy romp. Although Chaucer himself was a religious man, he attributes the fruity language in his text to the diversity of the characters on his pilgrimage, and argues, in the General Prologue, that he needs to 'speke hir [their] wordes proprely' (i.e., in character) in order to tell their tales (nice excuse, Geoff).

Herbert Starr, the literary critic, calculated that there are over two hundred different 'oaths' in *The Canterbury Tales*. Indeed, some of the more vulgar characters release veritable torrents of blasphemy that, while they may no longer be shocking today, would have been more disturbing to medieval readers than sexual innuendo or blue language – the Church was a central part of life in the fourteenth century. 'God's arms!', 'Christ's Passion!' and 'Benedictee!' are among the exclamations which would have appalled a contemporary audience – no less his use of 'for Goddes sake!'

Chaucer's swearing is much more shocking to a modern-day reader when relating to sexual matters, particularly his frequent references to genitalia. Even the dreaded 'cunt' appears, albeit with its archaic spelling of 'queynte'. In 'The Miller's Tale' a scene of flirtation advances a tad when 'prively he caughte hir by the queynte.' In 'The Wife of Bath's Tale', the Wife tells her betrothed:

For, certeyn, olde dotard, by youre leve
Ye shul have queynte right ynough at eve

In 'The Pardoner's Tale', the language of the Host, who is arguing with the Pardoner, becomes lavatorial in the extreme:

Thou woldest make me kisse thyn olde breech [trousers]
And swere it were a relyk of a seint
Though it were with thy fundement [shit] depeint!
But, by the croys which that Seint Eleyne fond
I wolde I hadde thy coillons [testicles] in myn hond

. . . .

They shul be shryned in an hogges toord! [turd]

The use of sexual puns was a common way of being saucy without using overtly sexual words. For example, the Shipman ends his tale by equating financial balance sheets with bed sheets, and wishing the pilgrims 'multiple entries'. He then goes on to say:

Thus endeth my tale, and God us sende
Taillynge ynough unto oure lyves ende. Amen.

Here Chaucer is playing on the ambiguity of 'taille', which in the fourteenth century could also refer to the female genitalia – the double entendre is clear.

Finally, it hardly needs to be said that Chaucer had a great line in insults, many of which we use today as extremely mild abuse but, to his audience, would have been more scandalous. Words such as 'lousy', 'idiot', 'shrew' and 'swine' were barely heard of before Chaucer put them down on the page, and would certainly have caused a stir among his contemporaries.

Derivation: 'Shit'

a) noun – excrement
b) verb – to defecate

'Shit' and 'Shite' have been in the English language since Anglo Saxon times, and as well as their literal sense are now used to mean 'rubbish' ('that's shit'), a bad person ('he's a shit') or drugs ('have you got any shit?')

The word appeared as early as the thirteenth century and some wonderful variations have appeared in the following centuries. In 1598 John Florio defined the term as 'A hot, violent fellow – a shit-fire', while in 1769 Francis Grose defined 'Shit-sack' as 'a dastardly fellow'.

Incidentally, the old English word for a heron was 'shiterow'.

Variations include: bullshit (often shortened to 'bull'), chickenshit, dipshit, gobshite, hot shit, shit-hot, (scared) shitless, shitting bricks, shit-faced, shitty

William 'the bawdy bard' Shakespeare

By the sixteenth century, when Shakespeare was putting quill to parchment, attitudes to swearing were once again changing and the censorship of obscenity, particularly on the stage, was beginning to be enforced with laws and heavy fines. Fortunately, while the censors may have been pious, they don't appear to have been very bright! Willy, being the cunning linguist (sorry, couldn't resist it!) that he was, often steered clear of outright swearing, but he still managed to sneak in the odd rude word here and there. In *Hamlet*, the phrase 'country matters' as used in the following exchange between Hamlet and Ophelia, suggests the C-word without actually saying it:

> *HAMLET: Lady, shall I lie in your lap?*
> *OPHELIA: No, my Lord.*
> *HAMLET: I mean, my head upon your lap?*
> *OPHELIA: Ay, my lord.*
> *HAMLET: Do you think I meant country matters?*
> *OPHELIA: I think nothing, my lord.*
> *HAMLET: That's a fair thought to lie between maids' legs.*

When Ophelia goes mad following her rejection by Hamlet, her language becomes increasingly foul mouthed; here, for example, she slips in a 'cock' (sorry again!), and her implied meaning is quite clear:

> *By Gis and by Saint Charity*
> *Alack, and fie for shame!*
> *Young men will do 't, if they come to 't*
> *By cock, they are to blame.*

Shakespeare would also embed profanity by writing it in another language. In *Henry V*, for example, he gets away with some surprisingly blue chitchat between the French princess Katherine and Alice, her lady-in-waiting, who is teaching her rudimentary English:

> *KATHERINE: Comment appelez-vous le pied et la robe?*
> *ALICE: Le foot, madame, et le count.*
> *KATHERINE: Le foot, et de count? O Seigneur Dieu! Ils sont mots de son mauvais, corruptible, gros, et impudique, et non pour le dames d'honneur d'user . . .*

The words Alice utters are innocent enough, but the French princess is outraged, claiming them inappropriate for ladies of honour to say. For, as those who understand French would have known, Katherine mistakenly hears *foot* and *count* as *foutre*, meaning 'fuck', and *con*, meaning 'cunt'.

'Bum' was one of Shakespeare's favourite words and he used it to great effect. In *Measure for Measure*, Escalus asks Pompey, the clown, what his surname is. 'Bum, sir', replies Pompey. To which Escalus quips, 'Troth, and your bum is the greatest thing about you; so that in the beastliest sense, you are Pompey the Great.'

Insults in Shakespearian plays were often long and poetic, but he could imbue them with every ounce of the vehemence and hatred in the worst invectives used today. In *King Lear*, Kent verbally abuses Oswald with an imaginative list of names, and in doing so creates the predecessor to the now-popular 'son of a bitch'. Oswald, he says, is . . .

> *A knave; a rascal; an eater of broken meats; a base, proud, shallow, beggarly, three-suited, hundred-pound, filthy, worsted-stocking knave; a lily-livered, action-taking knave, a whoreson, glass-gazing, superserviceable finical rogue; one-trunk-inheriting slave; one that wouldst be a bawd, in way of good service, and art nothing but the composition of a knave, beggar, coward, pandar, and the son and heir of a mongrel bitch . . .*

Dr Thomas 'stuffed-shirt' Bowdler

Born in 1734 to a pretty straight-laced family, Dr Thomas Bowdler and his equally sniffy sister Henrietta were brought up learning Shakespeare at their father's knee. Dad, however, took care to take all the rude words out as he read to his impressionable children so, when Henrietta and Thomas grew up, they decided to carry on the family tradition in printed form. Many scholars now believe that Henrietta produced the first version of *The Family Shakespeare* in 1807, but left her name off the book in case anyone should think that she understood the lewd terms which she edited out in the first place! Her brother, who was to become more famous, extended it for the 1818 edition from which, the preface announced, 'Those words and expressions are omitted which cannot with propriety be read aloud in a family.' After his death in 1825, Dr Bowdler's butchery of the text gave rise to the verb 'to Bowdlerize', meaning to remove material that is offensive or improper from a text, often with the connotation of weakening the work in the process.

Of Shakespeare's work, the Bowdler version cuts several lines in the first scene of *Othello* – Iago's famous encounter with Brabantio – lines such as: 'I am one, sir, that comes to tell you your daughter and the Moor are now making the beast with two backs,' as well as, 'Even now, now, very now, an old black ram is tupping your white ewe.' Some of the best lines, in other words! Strangely, however, 'impudent strumpet!' and 'cunning whore of Venice' survived the cut. Lady Macbeth's 'out damned spot!' became 'out crimson spot!' Juliet's speech, in which she declares her love for Romeo, was cut in half, and King Lear's insane rant ('Ay, every inch a king . . .') was reduced from twenty-two lines to seven. And Hamlet's 'bloody, bawdy villain' became 'bloody, murderous villain'. Silly sods.

Laurence 'sly' Sterne

In his multivolume work *The Life and Opinions of Tristram Shandy, Gentleman* (published between 1759 and 1767), the salacious Laurence Sterne got around the sensibilities of the day (and, perhaps, the demands of his own early calling as a county pastor) by merely hinting at vulgarity. When the incompetent Dr Slop cuts his thumb, and then overreacts to the incident,

Tristram's father chides him for unthinking use of 'small curses
. . . upon great occasions'.

> *I have the greatest veneration in the world for that*
> *gentleman who, in distrust of his own discretion in this*
> *point, sat down and composed (that is at his leisure) fit*
> *forms of swearing suitable to all cases, from the lowest to*
> *the highest provocations which could possibly happen to*
> *him – which forms . . . he kept ever by him on the chimney*
> *piece, within his reach, ready for use.*

He also creates an absurd situation involving two French nuns
who are stuck in a bog (don't ask), whose only chance of rescue
is if their two mules can pull them out. Unfortunately, the beasts
are stubborn and refuse to help. Then one of the nuns
remembers that mules often respond to rude words, but neither
is keen to speak such language for fear of eternal damnation. '[A]
French post-horse would not know what in the world to do, was
it not for the two words ****** and ****** in which there is as
much sustenance, as if you gave him a peck of corn,' she says.
Unfortunately, the only words that work are *bouger* and *foutre*
('bugger' and 'fuck'), and the nuns contrive to get over their
embarrassment – and eternal damnation – by uttering one
syllable each; from there, of course, the comic scene writes itself.

> *Abbess: bou . . . bou . . . bou . . .*
> *Margarita: ger . . . ger . . . ger . . .*

In fact, Sterne mistranslated the word *bouger*, either by mistake or
(more likely) on purpose as part of the general nonsense of jokes in
Tristram Shandy. *Bouger* actually means 'to move', the English
word 'budge' being derived from it, so it would have been perfectly
acceptable for the nuns to say this to the horse. The French word
bougre, cunningly close to *bouger*, can be taken to mean 'bugger'.

Dr Johnson's Dictionary

Like most great publishing ideas, Dr Samuel Johnson's pioneering dictionary, published in 1755, was conceived in a pub. The eighteenth-century egghead met a consortium of publishers over breakfast at the Golden Anchor near Holborn Bar in London, in 1746, and the good doctor accepted £1,575 (around £100,000 today) to produce a comprehensive dictionary.

His scrupulous research occupied almost ten years of his life, while his wife, Elizabeth Porter, spent most of her time drunk in bed and finally died of an overdose in 1752. Nonetheless, when it was completed in 1755, Johnson had produced – almost single-handedly – an impressive tome containing 42,773 entries. It wasn't the first English dictionary, as is commonly thought, but its innovation was in illustrating the meaning of words through literary quotations.

Happily, 'bum', 'fart', 'arse', and 'piss' all made it in to the dictionary, but an odd puritanical streak in Johnson led to him leave out 'shit', 'twat' and 'fuckwit', the latter apparently a favourite expression of the famous diarist, Samuel Pepys. Johnson did include, however, such marvellous terms as 'giglet' ('a wanton, lascivious girl'), 'fopdoodle' ('a fool'), and 'jobbernowl' ('a block head'); so, if you're ever stuck for a good insult, take a look at Johnson's book.

On the publication of his labour of love, a well-to-do lady congratulated him on keeping 'low' words out of his dictionary. In response, Johnson teased her for having looked them up! Despite omitting some of the more heinous profanities, it would seem that Johnson was no prude in person. When asked what his chief pleasure in life was he answered, 'Fucking, and the second is drinking', and went on to marvel that there were not more drunkards in the world 'for all could drink though all could not fuck'.

Not long after the publication of Johnson's dictionary the aptly named Francis Grose produced his own version, with a unique twist – it was titled *A Classical Dictionary of the Vulgar Tongue* (1785). This included many of the words Johnson had left out, and a few more besides. Some of the more colourful phrases include 'shit sack', defined as 'a dastardly fellow', and 'shitting through the teeth' – vomiting. Another word for a valet or footman is 'fart catcher' (from the fact they would walk behind their master or mistress), and 'fartleberries' (my personal favourite) are described as 'excrement hanging about the anus'. Nice!

In fairness, Dr Johnson wasn't the only dictionary compiler to leave out the rude bits. In fact, the *Oxford English Dictionary* didn't include the words 'fuck' and 'cunt' until the early 1970s, when progressive editor Robert Burchfield opted to include them. In a later article he recalled that, having included the words in an *Oxford English Dictionary* supplement, he sent the draft to the Bodleian Library for verification. 'I was told by the library research assistant at the time that she had had "quite enough of the kind of filth found in Partridge and other dictionaries of slang". It seemed tactful not to insist and I therefore had the doubtful privilege of looking out the material myself.'

George Bernard 'bloody' Shaw

On 11 April 1914, George Bernard Shaw's play *Pygmalion* opened at His Majesty's Theatre, Haymarket, London, amid huge scandal. The play is the story of a cockney flower girl who is taught to speak perfect English by a language professor trying to win a bet. Shaw wrote the play for a Mrs Patrick Campbell, with whom he was passionately in love, and who thanked him 'for thinking I can play your pretty little slut'.

Even before the first curtain had gone up the press had gotten wind of the offensive language it contained, and a national debate was raging. The *Daily Sketch* ran an article about 'the forbidden word' and asked, 'Will Mrs Patrick Campbell Speak It?' The word, it claimed, was 'expected to cause the biggest theatre sensation for many years'. It was referred to in other papers as 'Shaw's Big Bold Word', 'The Unprintable Swearword', and 'The "Langwidge" of the Flower Girl'.

On the night of the first performance the press swarmed to the theatre and waited in anticipation. When Campbell did pronounce the 'incarnadine adverb' (as *The Daily Mail* pompously referred to it), there was a few seconds of 'stunned, unbelieving silence' and then over a minute of hysterical laughter. Shaw was horrified by the response and stormed from the theatre.

In the following week the word was denounced by preachers and politicians alike. *The Daily Express* even took a genuine flower girl to the play and then quoted her as saying that the language was shocking and that no proper cockney flower girl would say such a thing.

And the scandalous line was? 'Walk! Not bloody likely.'

Bernard Shaw himself responded to the outrage by issuing a statement for the *Daily News*: 'I have nothing particular to say about Eliza Doolittle's language. I do not know anything more ridiculous than the refusal of some newspapers (at several pages' length) to print the word "bloody", which is in common use as an expletive by four-fifths of the English nation, including many highly educated persons.'

In New York, when the play transferred, the word caused very little reaction in the theatre and seems to have been regarded by most as quaint English slang. *Pygmalion* went on to become George Bernard Shaw's most famous and celebrated play, and later spawned the hit musical *My Fair Lady*.

D. H. 'loverboy' Lawrence

Famously filthy minded, Lawrence bit off more than he could chew when he wrote *Lady Chatterley's Lover*. In a previous edition the novel had been called *John Thomas and Lady Jane*, but Lawrence would eventually change its name, partly as a result of realizing the social and political storm his story of a lowly gardener's affair with his aristocratic mistress would brew. While writing the work he described it to a friend as 'the most improper book ever written, but would always refute the accusation that it was just pornography. First published in Florence in 1928, *Lady Chatterley's Lover* was the first serious work of English literature to contain the word 'fuck' in reference to copulation; for good measure, it also included several 'cunts'.

By the following year several editions had found their way to America and Europe and the backlash was in full swing.

An article in the English magazine *John Bull* denounced the book as 'the most evil outpouring that has ever besmirched the literature of this country' and declared that 'the creations of muddy minded perverts, peddled in the back-street book stalls of Paris, are prudish by comparison.' Other publications condemned the book as 'the abysm of filth' and 'the foulest book in English literature', which probably made people want to rush out and buy it even more. But the call for circulation to be stopped was heeded and the book was banned. Lawrence, after attempting to cut out the rude bits, gave up. 'I might as well try to clip my own nose into shape with scissors. The book bleeds.'

Some thirty years later, in 1959, American publishers Grove Press won a US court case and were allowed to publish *Lady Chatterley's Lover* in the States. In the same year, Penguin Books attempted to publish the novel in Britain, but were instantly charged under the Obscene Publications Act of 1959. The subsequent court case, *Regina Vs Penguin Books, Ltd,* in 1960, has become one of the most famous court cases of the century, and its landmark ruling changed the landscape of what was deemed acceptable publishing. Witnesses for the defence included E. M. Forster, Richard Hoggart, Kenneth Muir and the Bishop of Woolwich – figures from all walks of life, who were all willing to testify to the work's intrinsic artistic and creative merits.

One passage discussed in the courtroom has the gardener Mellors explaining the C-word to Lady Jane, in his distinctive broad dialect:

> 'Th'art good cunt, though, aren't ter? Best bit o'cunt left on earth. When ter likes! When tha'rt willing!'
> 'What is cunt?' she said.
> 'An'doesn't ter know? Cunt! It's thee down theer; an' what I get when I'm i'side thee; it's a' as it is, all on't.'
> 'All on't,' she teased. 'Cunt! It's like fuck then.'
> 'Nay nay! Fuck's only what you do. Animals fuck. But cunt's a lot more than that. It's thee, dost see: an tha'rt a lot besides an animal, aren't ter? – even ter fuck? Cunt! Eh, that's the beauty o' thee, lass!'

Mr Mervyn Griffiths-Jones, the prosecuting council, asked the jury the somewhat pompous question: 'Is this a book you would wish your wife or servants to read?', which, it is speculated, displayed the court's old-fashioned values and possibly swayed the jury to a 'not guilty' verdict. Sure enough, the expensive and lengthy trial ended with Penguin Books being acquitted and the ban on the novel was overturned. With the publicity surrounding the trial amounting to the best advertising campaign a publisher could hope for, *Lady Chatterley's Lover* sold over 3 million copies in the next two years, and can still be found in every bookshop across the land.

The *Oz* Trial

The effect of 'the Lady C trial' was an explosion of uncensored media and literary expression that led to many taboos being broken in print. Theatre and literature became more outrageous and new magazines with titles such as *Screw*, *Suck* and even *Cunts and Grunts*, emerged. At the same time, a growing desire

Derivation: 'Sod'

a) noun – turf
b) noun – an unpleasant person

As well as being used as an insult, this word can also mean 'a rotter' or 'a cad', hence the apocryphal story about the epitaph that reads 'Under this sod, lies another'. Originally, however, 'sod' is a contraction of 'sodomite' – someone who engages in anal sex. 'Sodomite' itself derives from the Old Testament story in Genesis in which God destroys the city of Sodom (and Gomorrah) because of the sinful behaviour of its residents.

Oscar Wilde fell foul of the law thanks to this word. The Marquis of Queensberry, the father of Wilde's lover Lord Alfred Douglas, accused Wilde of being a 'somdomite' (*sic*). Rather inadvisably, Wilde decided to sue for libel, but when it was revealed that the Marquis was actually correct, Wilde himself was convicted and sentenced to imprisonment.

Variations include: sodding, sod it, sod's law, sod all, sod this for a game of soldiers

to stem the tide of 'filth' culminated in 1971 when the publishers of the satirical magazine *Oz* found themselves in court charged with obscenity.

The subversive magazine boasted that its values were 'dope, rock'n'roll and fucking in the streets'; its articles advocated free sex, antiestablishment sentiment, and it ran campaigns to discredit the police and the judiciary. It is not surprising, therefore, that the judge hearing the case wasn't too sympathetic!

The trial centred on the *School Kids Issue: Oz 28*, which advocated guerrilla action against schools, showed a portrait of a schoolboy and schoolmaster after a blow job, and showed a cartoon of Rupert the Bear having sex with 'Gipsy Granny'. Obviously, there was also a fair amount of profanity scattered through the publication. Judge Michael Argyle QC was so enraged by *Oz* that he sentenced the editor, Richard Neville, to fifteen months in prison, while his associates (one of whom was Felix Dennis, now multimillionaire and publisher of mags such as *Maxim* and *Viz*) received twelve and nine months for their crimes.

The sentences, later overturned, were extremely harsh – but that's what you get when you fuck with the guys in wigs!

J. D. 'goddamn' Salinger

The Catcher in the Rye is J. D. Salinger's most famous novel, and from its first publication in 1951 it split American opinion. Although many hailed it as a great novel, the disturbing story of troubled teenager Holden Caulfield caused outrage across the States because of its offensive language and its references to premarital sex, alcohol abuse and prostitution.

In 1957, a shipment of the novels destined as a gift to the Australian government from the US Ambassador was seized by Australian customs. When the shipment was finally released it was with an accompanying note saying that the book contained obscene language and references to inappropriate behaviour. In 1960, an Oklahoma teacher was sacked for assigning the book to his teenaged English class, but on appeal he was reinstated. The book was not permitted to return with the teacher!

The Catcher in the Rye became the most frequently banned book in schools between 1966 and 1975, and, in 1978, in one of many such incidents in the last fifty years, irate parents in Issaquah, Washington, counted 785 uses of profanity as proof that it should be proscribed.

In fact, objections to the lurid language carried on throughout the eighties and nineties and, even now, fifty years after its publication, there is the still the occasional call for it to be banished from the classroom. The amazing thing is that, while the book details an instance of graffiti reading 'Fuck You', the profanities are mainly limited to Holden's frequent outbursts of 'goddamn!' and 'damn!' which, outside of the US 'Bible belt', seem pretty tame.

Incidentally, the book has had other, weirder, associations. Mark Chapman was carrying a copy of the book when he assassinated John Lennon, and referred to it in his statement to police, although no psychological link could be found between the book and Chapman's actions. In the 1997 film *Conspiracy Theory*, Mel Gibson's paranoid character Jerry Fletcher believes Government agencies use the book to brainwash, and buys every copy he sees while refusing to read it.

Philip 'they fuck you up' Larkin

Philip Larkin was perhaps an unlikely champion of the swear word. Born in 1922, he was a speccy Oxford graduate who spent much of his life as a librarian in Hull, writing poetry and novels in his spare time.

An award-winning poet, whose work includes 'Aubade', 'The Old Fools' and the collection *High Windows* (1974), Larkin was a quiet man who preferred to stay out of the spotlight. In 1984, when offered the chance to succeed Sir John Betjeman as Poet Laureate, he declined, claiming that he wouldn't be comfortable with such a public position. Larkin, who died of cancer in 1985, used his language carefully, but didn't flinch from using profanity to convey his point. Even in the early 1970s, when the F-word was still capable of causing moral outrage, he used it in the first line of the now-famous poem 'This Be The Verse'. Frankly, there was no better way to say what he had to say! The two extracts below demonstrate his use of 'fuck':

> *They fuck you up, your mum and dad.*
> *They may not mean to, but they do.*
> 'THIS BE THE VERSE' (1971)

> *When I see a couple of kids*
> *And guess he's fucking her . . .*
> 'HIGH WINDOWS' (1974)

These extracts demonstrate the power of invective language when used skilfully and appropriately; it has the ability to get to the heart of the matter.

The 'Blank', Mrs Beeton and the Asterisk

In nineteenth-century polite society, swear words were no longer in favour and all but the boldest contemporary writers shied away from bad language. Hence the word 'blank' became the 'expletive deleted' and was used as a replacement for any strong word. The *Oxford English Dictionary* cites the example, recorded in 1908, of people cursing 'this blankety blank train', which also goes to show that public transport was just as likely to cause angry outbursts then as it is now.

Mrs Beeton, the domestic goddess of her day and author of the classic *Mrs Beeton's Book of Household Management* (1861), found her own way of replacing the words she couldn't bring herself to put into print – words which included 'trousers'! For example, writing about how a valet should dress his master she referred to that particular item of clothing as 'the unmentionables', 'the indescribables' and 'the inexplicable'.

The practice of using the asterisk to tone down an offending word in print ('f***ing c**t', for example) was actually established in the early eighteenth century, but is still seen in many publications, especially tabloid newspapers, to this day. The recent reports on the alleged relationship between David Beckham and Rebecca Loos, for example, had many a tabloid reader desperately trying to guess the content of their graphic text messages as the majority of the letters were replaced with asterisks!

These are some of the messages reported in *The News of the World* in April 2004. See if you can work them out!

DAVID BECKHAM (DB): Next time it will be ****er and **tter and all ****** you.

REBECCA LOOS (RL): Stop you are driving me wild I really want you now.

DB: . . . and all over your **** and ****.

RL: You can **** all **** me and I'll **** it *** with pleasure . . . Just let me know when . . . am looking forward to it.

DB: Me too. Can't tell you how much I just ***.

Derivation: 'Piss'

a) noun – urine
b) verb – to pass water

A great onomatopoeic word, 'piss' (Scottish 'pish') comes from the Latin *pissare*, and Old French *pisser*.

In the seventeenth and eighteenth centuries, an arrogant gentleman may have been described as 'piss-proud'; referring to the fact that men can wake up in the morning with erections caused by the pressure of the bladder on the prostate. A 1725 dictionary described a 'vain-glorious or ostentatious' man as 'One that boasts without reason, or, as the Canters say, "pisses more than he drinks".'

The word has become integral to many common English phrases. If you ridicule someone you 'take the piss'; mucking about can be described as 'pissing about', and when it is raining heavily it is 'pissing down'. To get drunk is to 'get pissed'; to go for a drinking session is to 'go out on the piss' with the usual result of 'pissing it against a wall', or wasting your money. A common phrase for an inept person is someone who 'couldn't organize a piss-up in a brewery'.

Chamber pots used to be known as 'pisspots' and the Old English name for the dandelion was 'pissabed', as it was known to have diuretic qualities.

Variations include: piss off, pissed off, pissed up, pissing, pissy, pisshead, piss-poor, piece of piss, piss-take, pisser, piss artist, pissing in the wind

Famous Foul-mouths: Celebrity Chefs

The late nineties and early 2000s saw the rise of the 'celebrity chef', and no one can be in any doubt that when the kitchen is red hot, the language turns blue! Gary Rhodes and Jean-Christophe Novelli were seen to pepper their kitchens with more than condiments in the recent programme Hell's Kitchen, and many of the new breed of saucepan supremos react to stress by hurling a stream of obscenities. Even 'Saint' Jamie Oliver got into trouble with some viewers for saying, 'I want us to have a fucking better, cooler, cleverer, healthier nation' in his School Dinners show (although Ofcom backed him on that one).

While the likes of Nico Ladenis and Marco Pierre White are famed for their tempers, they have confined their outbursts to their kitchens or, on one or two occasions, directed them at their diners. However, the popularity of 'celebrity chef' television programmes has brought their choice language into the living rooms of the nation.

As the somewhat calmer cook Clarissa Dickson Wright so perfectly put it in a recent newspaper article, 'Chefs are attention-seeking, adrenalin junkies. Put that on reality television and what do you expect?'

Gordon Ramsay

The king of the kitchen cursers, Gordon can barely bark an order at an underling without using a four-letter word. A Scottish chef who trained under Marco Pierre White and Albert Roux, among others, Ramsey got his first big break in the restaurant business when he became the part owner of Aubergine in London where he gained two Michelin stars. After falling out with the restaurant's backers (and undoubtedly swearing a lot), he left to set up his own restaurant in Chelsea, called, imaginatively, Gordon Ramsay. Perhaps surprisingly, considering the amount of times he swears at them, his staff came with him. He now has restaurants in the Connaught, Claridge's, at the Berkeley Hotel in Knightsbridge, and even in Dubai (called Verre).

His recent TV programmes, including *Hell's Kitchen* and *Ramsay's Kitchen Nightmares*, have seen such a string of foul language that he has banned his children from watching Daddy on TV. A source said, 'He won't be letting them watch it because of the agricultural nature of his language.' One episode of *Ramsay's Kitchen Nightmares* contained 111 swear words.

In 2004, Gordon was the subject of a complaint to Ofcom after an estimated 5,000 swear words throughout the first series of *Hell's Kitchen*. Ofcom rejected the complaint regarding the persistent swearing, but ruled that Ramsay had breached acceptable standards by coupling the word 'fucking' with 'Jesus', saying, 'Strong swearing coupled directly with holy names is found highly offensive by believers.'

Ironically, when Channel Four asked him to present the show *The F Word* (the 'F-word' being 'food', incidentally), they informed him that, as it was to be screened at 8 p.m. – an hour before the watershed – he wouldn't be allowed to swear. Gordon's characteristic response?

'We're fucked then, aren't we?'

Gary Rhodes

Gary Rhodes and his *Hell's Kitchen* co-star Jean-Christophe Novelli both suffer from a short fuse, so sparks were bound to fly when they went head to head in a 'cook off'.

The 2005 series saw each chef running his own kitchen along with five apprentice chefs fighting for orders from a restaurant full of celebrity diners. Before the show even started Gary Rhodes promised there would be plenty of foul language in his kitchen.

'I'll be like Alex Ferguson,' said Gary. 'If my team does well they get a pat on the back. If they don't, they take a bollocking.

'You'll be seeing a different Gary Rhodes. People who fart about, or fall asleep on the job: I'll be shouting at them, "Fucking wake up!" I'm only a nice bloke at home. At work I take on a different personality.'

Gary, who has proved the point about being a nice bloke at home by staying married to wife Jenny for twenty-six years, knew he wanted to be a chef at the age of fourteen, when he cooked a Sunday roast for his family. He gained his first Michelin star at the Castle Hotel in Somerset, and not long afterwards shot to fame in such series as *Rhodes Around Britain* and *Gary Rhodes at the Table*.

Although his earlier TV shows were profanity-free, *Hell's*

Kitchen was to be a different experience, with Rhodes's constant swearing, shouting at his staff and being incredibly rude about his French rival.

On the first night of the competition the two chefs had an almighty row in which Gary Rhodes accused Novelli of behaving badly. An anonymous member of the production team, quoted in *The Daily Mirror*, said, 'After a stressful night they were shouting and swearing at each other. They made Gordon Ramsay sound like Fanny Cradock.'

As the evenings went on and the pressure got to Gary, his team suffered a stream of abuse – including the immortal line, 'That's not a spatula, that's a fucking whisk!' But the Kent chef reckons that the mildest of men can turn into foul-mouthed fiends when they're cooking.

'Any chef who tells you they haven't sworn in the kitchen is an out-and-out liar. We all swear in the kitchen.'

Jean-Christophe Novelli

The smouldering good looks and smooth French accent of Jean-Christophe Novelli has earned him the reputation as the heart-throb of the catering world. Once voted the World's Sexiest Man by *The New York Times*, he has famously compared cooking to sex, prompting the barbed comment from Gary Rhodes: 'Jean-Christophe is always saying that cooking is like making love, but with his food, the foreplay might be great, but when you eat it you're still waiting for the orgasm.'

Before taking on Gary Rhodes in *Hell's Kitchen*, the chef from Arras in France told the press, 'I wake up every morning and I want to kiss the world. I want to kiss everybody around. I don't want to fight or argue. I think life is too short.' The fans who tuned in to watch, therefore, understandably expected the Gallic charm of a man who compares cooking to sex to provide a stark contrast to the down-to-earth language of rival Gary Rhodes. They were *so* wrong.

On the first day the smooth-talking chef unleashed a tirade at hapless trainee Henry Filoux Bennett, leaving him in tears. The Nottingham student had committed the unforgivable crime of putting beef stock in a vegetarian dish and the Frenchman smashed both plate and food against the wall, shouting, 'Get out of the kitchen. Get the fuck out of here!' before sending a rack of utensils crashing to the floor.

His abuse of poor Henry continued. 'We should have been winning – our standard was better – and we fucked up on that one thing and that's what pissed me off. This was a disgusting fucking plate he made. The reason I lost it is because he didn't share his problem. I don't mind people fucking up if they share it. He fucked up and last minute we found out.'

In fact, Jean-Christophe even managed to swear while *complimenting* one of Rhode's bread-and-butter puddings. 'This is nice. You bastard! It's gorgeous. Why am I sitting here giving you compliments? Because it's actually fantastic. I've got to give you that.'

It's not surprising perhaps that with the air thick with invectives, it wasn't only the chefs whose language got spicy. One of the trainees, Stein Smart, was asked to leave after he threatened Jean-Christophe on the show.

'If he wants to go toe-to-toe,' Smart said, 'that's fine. I'll knock the cunt out.'

Smart explained his outburst by telling the other contestants, 'I was that close to breaking his fucking nose and nutting him live on television. They pushed me too fucking far.'

Big (Blue) Screen

The last century has seen the cinema grow from a fledgling invention to a multi-billion-dollar international industry. Throughout its existence, the big screen has reflected the social mores, attitudes and beliefs of those making, and watching, its product. Invariably then, as societal attitudes to swearing have changed through time, opinions about profanity in films have shifted dramatically too.

In February 2005, after an extensive survey involving 11,000 people from across the UK, the British Board of Film Classification (the BBFC) found that racism and blasphemy had overtaken swearing as the main worry for parents taking their children to the cinema. In response to the survey, the BBFC announced new guidelines for restrictions on the age categories used to 'rate' films. For the first time, those swear words generally thought most offensive (the F- and C-words particularly) were more likely to be accepted in films approved for viewing by younger teenagers, especially when their context is humorous rather than violent. However, racially abusive terms were more likely to gain a film a 15 or an 18 rating.

The people who took part in the survey were asked to indicate which issues they found 'Very Important' as regards classification. Drugs and drug taking came first at 75 per cent, then violence (65 per cent), sex (56 per cent), followed by swearing (46 per cent). The Board also found growing concern over 'expletives with a racial association' which, along with 'incitement to racial violence' and 'language which offends vulnerable minorities', was given an increased emphasis. Although most people consider it fairly inoffensive, casual blasphemy, such as 'Jesus Christ' (used as an expletive), was now to be taken more seriously in the classification decisions.

The Board's director David Cooke said, 'We are acutely aware that there will be works which we pass, at whatever classification, which may shock or offend some sections of the population, just as we sometimes outrage libertarian views when we intervene to cut, or even refuse a certificate.'

Sue Clark, press officer for the BBFC, said that the days of films being banned for the use of swear words is in the past.

'A film is never banned because of bad language,' she says. 'Film producers are often advised to change some words if they want a lower certificate, or to accept a higher certificate. Usually it is cut or dubbed. For instance, *Bridget Jones's Diary* originally contained the C-word, and the BBFC told them that they would have to change it if they wanted a 15 certificate, so they changed it to "cow".'

There are other ways of getting round the problem too.

'If a subtitled film has a strong expletive, it will be changed in the translation but not dubbed, as the majority of British audiences won't know what it means.'

This attitude shows a huge shift towards institutional and public acceptance of foul language in films. In the 1930s the word 'damn' would cause worldwide controversy, but nowadays most Hollywood blockbusters are peppered with as many swear words as they are bullets. Exposure to more and more incidences of swearing renders an audience immune to their intended effect; to compensate, even more liberal use is made of them – a vicious circle.

Gone with the Wind

Recently voted the most memorable movie line ever, 'Frankly, my dear, I don't give a damn' caused uproar when it was first uttered by Clark Gable in the 1939 movie. During the making of *Gone With The Wind*, legendary producer David O. Selznick became embroiled in an argument with the Hays Office (an association that sought to enforce high moral standards in the US motion-picture industry). The Office were refusing to allow the word 'damn' to be screened, and suggested that the climactic scene of the epic movie should end with Rhett Butler saying 'Frankly, I don't care!' as he leaves Scarlett O'Hara for the last time. Selznick wrote to William Hayes about the matter; the following is an extract from his letter:

The word as used in the picture, is not an oath or a curse . . . The worst that could be said for it is that it is a vulgarism, and it is so described in the Oxford English Dictionary *. . . Nor do I feel that in asking you to make an*

exception in this case . . . this one sentence will open up
the floodgates. I do believe, however, that if you were to
permit our using this dramatic word in its rightfully
dramatic place, it would establish a helpful precedent . . .
giving your office discretionary powers to allow the use of
certain harmless oaths and ejaculations whenever they
are . . . not prejudicial to public morals. The omission of
this line spoils the punch at the very end of the picture
and on our very fadeout gives an impression of
unfaithfulness after three hours and forty-five minutes of
extreme fidelity to Miss Mitchell's work which has become
. . . an American Bible.

Hays overruled his board of advisers and the line was screened at the cinema. He then fined Selznick $15,000 for violating the Production Code.

I'll Never Forget What's'isname

The 1967 movie *I'll Never Forget What's'isname*, directed by Michael Winner, is credited with the first use of the word 'fuck' in the cinema. In fact the film was passed by the BBFC because of a very clever subterfuge that disguised the unacceptable language.

The hip drama starred Orson Welles and Oliver Reed, and tells the story of an advertising whizzkid (Reed) who chucks in his job and leaves his wife and mistresses behind to start a new life. The offending scene in question shows Marianne Faithfull, one of Reed's mistresses, screaming, 'Get out of here, you fucking bastard!' The expletive, however, is obscured by the sound of a car horn and the censors in the UK passed it.

The film attracted further controversy in the States where the MPAA (Motion Picture Association of America) denied the film their approval because of a scene between Oliver Reed and Carol

White that inferred an act of oral sex. Universal, through a subsidiary company, distributed it anyway.

Incidentally, Reed's character in the film is called 'Quint' – we all know what that would have meant to Geoffrey Chaucer.

Ulysses

In the same year as *I'll Never Forget What's'isname* was released, James Joyce's controversial masterpiece *Ulysses* was brought to the big screen by director Joseph Strick. The story of Stephen Dedalus (played by Martin Dempsey), a would-be Irish poet who spends a day wandering around Dublin with a new-found friend, Leopold Bloom (Milo O'Shea), caused controversy in the film world with the use of the word 'fuck'. The BBFC refused to pass the film unless cuts were made and the American director refused, calling the head of the BBFC, John Trevelyan, 'your friendly neighbourhood film mortician'.

However, encouraged by the film critic Derek Hill, who had previously shown his 'festival of forbidden films' at a cinema in Notting Hill, some authorities decided to show the film anyway. The BBFC sent local authorities extracts from the script and fifty-six councils rejected it, while twenty-six chose to screen it. In Southampton, where the film was banned, Alderman Michael Petit, the Chairman of the Public Safety Committee, commented that he had read the book and 'without its obscenities and blasphemies a film version of *Ulysses* wouldn't be worth seeing anyway.'

In New Zealand, the film was deemed so controversial and 'an embarrassment for mixed company to view' that it could only be screened before gender-segregated audiences; in Ireland it was banned until September 2000.

Derivation: 'Bastard'

a) noun – an illegitimate or nasty person.

The origin of 'bastard' is thought to be the French term *fils de bast* meaning 'son of the packsaddle', the implication being that the child has been born out of wedlock.

The term has been around for over a thousand years. Illegitimate invader William the Conqueror was known as 'William the Bastard' until the Battle of Hastings in 1066 earned him his more complimentary title. When Lord Mountbatten met his death at the hands of the IRA in 1979, one tabloid headline, on the front page, denounced the killers as 'Murdering Bastards'.

In the UK 'bastard' can be used as both an insult or in a more affectionate way, e.g. 'you old bastard' or 'you lucky bastard'. It can also be used to describe both a thing that is causing problems or is difficult to do, as in 'this sore knee is a bastard' or 'cleaning that table was a bastard'.

'Bastard' has also given us the verb 'to bastardize', meaning to debase something or to make it illegitimate.

Four Weddings and a Funeral

The highest-grossing British film of the twentieth century opens with a stream of F-words from Hugh Grant, who, as the beleaguered Charles, wakes up to find he is late for a wedding.

And, with the memorably alliterative line, 'Fuck, fuck, fuckety-fuck fuck!', the screenwriters coined a further derivation of the endlessly versatile F-word, one that has now moved into the English language ('fuckety-fuck'!)

In fact, by the nineties, it was becoming much more acceptable to swear in mainstream cinema. One of the things that made *Four Weddings and a Funeral* so memorable was that despite the fact it was a romantic comedy, a British film and, more importantly, the sort of 'sweet' film you could take your mum to, it could also contain this form of humorous profanity. Countless viewers must have squirmed in front of the cinema screen or the telly (as I did), having told your mum, your granny and your mother-in-law that they'll love this film, only to realize you had forgotten that the first five words all began with 'F'. Perhaps it could be said that the film did much to advance the acceptance of the F-word in contexts other than the shoot-'em-up cop movies it littered before. Hugh Grant's pleasantly plummy accent rendered his swearing inoffensive and comical.

Other great lines from the film: Charles's exclamation of 'fuck-a-doodle-doo!'; and his reaction to seeing the true love of his life, Carrie (played by Andie MacDowell), turn up at his wedding as he's getting married to Henrietta (aka Duckface). 'Dear Lord, forgive me for what I am about to, ah, say in this magnificent place of worship . . . Bugger! Bugger! Bugger, bugger, bugger, bugger!'

When the producers were asked to make a TV version for America they chose to reshoot every scene that contained an instance of offensive language rather than overdub. 'Bugger' replaced 'fuck' throughout. When George explains to Charles how he went to school with the groom's brother who 'buggered me senseless', the American TV version became 'beat me till my bottom turned blue'. Finally, and rather sadly, Charles's 'fuck-a-doodle-doo!' was toned down beyond recognition (and comedy) to 'well, that's that, then.'

Reservoir Dogs

Quentin Tarantino's directorial debut blasted onto the cinema screen in 1992 and created shockwaves throughout the movie world. The gangster flick, which Tarantino also wrote, is about a gang of thieves who carry out an armed robbery on a diamond warehouse, but who are immediately set upon by the police. Convinced they have a traitor in their midst they set about discovering the mole, primarily through the use of violence and torture.

The stylish but shocking content of *Reservoir Dogs* made the film an instant cult hit and turned Tarantino into the hottest director in Hollywood. This also meant the average swear count in Tinseltown shot up overnight.

The film contains 252 uses of the word 'fuck', which, when it was screened on Channel Four gave it the record for the greatest number of profanities in a single show on British TV – until the broadcast of *Jerry Springer – The Opera*.

Excessive swearing and violence were to become a trademark of Quentin Tarantino's films. *True Romance*, which he wrote but didn't direct, contained 225 uses of 'fuck' or its derivatives, while the 1994 smash-hit *Pulp Fiction* contained 271.

However his 2003 film *Kill Bill: Volume 1* brought a sea change as it contained only seventeen expletives, and, according to actor David Carradine, swearing was banned on-set in order to protect the child stars of the film and the younger visitors to the set. Of one particular girl, Carradine said:

'There was a penalty for swearing around her. When I found out, I said, "You mean there's a way I can get off this movie?"'

'Quentin Tarantino said, "No, it'll just cost you ten bucks!"'

Some *Reservoir Dogs* quotes:

Mr Orange: *Fuck you! Fuck you! I'm fucking dying here! I'm fucking dying!*

Mr Pink: *Man, this is fucked up. This is so fucked up. Somebody fucked us up big time, man.*

Some Pulp Fiction *quotes:*

Jules: *Look, just because I don't be givin' no man a foot massage don't make it right for Marsellus to throw Antwan into a glass motherfuckin' house fuckin' up the way the nigger talks. Motherfucker do that shit to me, he better paralyze my ass cuz I'll kill the motherfucker, know what I'm sayin'?*

Jules: *ENGLISH, MOTHERFUCKER! DO-YOU-SPEAK-IT?*

South Park

The fact that there was swearing in this 1999 film-cartoon came as no surprise to fans of the series, but *South Park: Bigger, Longer & Uncut* surpassed all expectation by landing itself in the book of *Guinness World Records*. As of 2005, the 80-minute film still held the record for the 'Most Swearing in an Animated Movie', with an incredible count of 399 – an irony in itself, as one of the show's central themes is swearing in films.

The film features a fictional popular comedy duo called Terrance and Phillip, whose innocuous-looking show is actually packed full of obscenity. When the South Park kids repeat the words they've heard at the cinema, their parents place Terrance and Phillip under citizens' arrest. It is up to the kids to save the world from Satan (and Saddam Hussein), and keep Terrance and Phillip from being executed.

Aside from the 399 instances of swearing (including 146 'fucks'), 199 offensive gestures were counted as well as 221 acts of violence.

Paramount originally asked *South Park* creators Trey Parker and Matt Stone if they could make a PG-13 rated film. They declined and would not agree to make a movie until the studio agreed that the final product would be rated R. They also enjoyed trying to cram in as many offensive words as possible.

'We'd try to get anything past the Motion Picture Association of America,' admitted Parker.

They did a good job. Among the highlights of the movie are the songs 'Uncle Fucka' (sung by Terrance and Phillip) and Cartman singing a song called 'Kyle's Mom's a bitch'.

Here are a few *South Park* swearing moments (and believe me there are many more to choose from) – the humour is very much of an acquired taste . . .

Terrance: *You're such a pig-fucker, Phillip!*
Phillip: *Terrance, why would you call me a pig-fucker?*
Terrance: *Well, let's see. First of all, you fuck pigs.*
Phillip: *Oh yeah!*

Mr Mackey: [singing] *Step 4 – don't say 'fuck' anymore,*
'cause 'fuck' is the worst word that you can say.
Children: *'Fuck' is the worst word that you can say. We*
shouldn't say 'fuck', no we shouldn't say 'fuck', fuck no!

[American representative stands up and clears his throat – then pauses]
American representative: *Fuck Canada!*
Canadian representative: *Hey, fuck you, buddy!*

Other Fucking Film Facts

At a London interview for his 2004 film *Polar Express*, Tom Hanks was getting hot under the collar about the US censorship of *Saving Private Ryan* for TV. He told the assembled journalists: 'ABC affiliates wouldn't run *Ryan* recently because of its use of the F-word and because they were scared of lawsuits. This is the same network that will put out *The Bachelor*, in which a guy essentially gets to fuck whatever girl he wants to until he decides which one to pick. Pardon my language.'

•

In 1999, British super-spy Austin Powers upset the censors in Thailand who thought *The Spy Who Shagged Me* was far too racy a title. Warner Bros's general manager in Singapore, Ken Low, told local press that the Thai Board of Film Censors had rejected the word 'Shagged' in the tile and submitted 'Shoiked' in its place. 'Shoiked' means 'good' or 'nice'. The film was released as *Austin Powers: The Spy Who Shoiked Me*.

•

Demi Moore came under fire in 1997 for her 'feminist fights back' film *GI Jane*. America's Baptist Church was unhappy with the amount of obscene language she used in her role as a tough naval officer. At one point in the film she 'screams out an anatomical obscenity' (which may refer to 'suck my dick!', shouted at her CO). The Church urged its members to boycott the film.

•

Weird as it may seem for a U-certificate animated film from Dreamworks, their 2005 summer hit *Madagascar* had to be cut before it could be passed by the BBFC. In one scene, Marty the Zebra, voiced by Chris Rock, cries out 'Motherf—' – at which point he is cut off mid-word by another conversation. Relaxed as the BBFC have become about swearing, they felt that, for a film aimed at children under ten, this was unacceptable.

•

In 2005, an American documentary was made entitled, simply, *Fuck*. The film is, the producers say, 'an examination of the four-letter word'. Before its completion, director Steve Anderson said that his film would be 'an honest look at the word, and will make room for all opinions to be heard'.

Soon showing in a multiplex near you – NOT!

●

Hollywood heart-throb Johnny Depp swapped his American twang for some Anglo-Saxon language when he took on the role of Lord Rochester in the 2005 movie *The Libertine*. The film, based on the life of the famous philanderer from the court of Charles II (see pages 12-13), is peppered with the C-word and caused some viewers at the Toronto Film Festival to walk out in disgust.

Depp's co-star John Malkovich, who also produced the film, was unfazed by the reaction to the language: 'The language was the language of the time and the language of the play. There are probably many things in the story that are stronger and more offensive than the language but that was the language utilized by Rochester and I can say that it never went through my mind or [director] Laurence Dunmore's mind that there was a reason to change it. I think it is very integral to this story.'

Dunmore himself explains that the two lead actors, both firm Francophiles in real life, had to call the French 'cunts' in the film.

'It wasn't hard to get either of them to say it, strangely enough,' laughed the director.

More Movie Mouth-offs

'What the fuck?!'
Opening line from *House of Games*

'That guy's a fuckin' asshole. Anybody who talks to that asshole is a fuckin' asshole.'
Ed Harris in *Glengarry Glen Ross*

'I may be a bastard, but I'm not a fucking bastard.'
George Clooney in *From Dusk 'Til Dawn*

'Another fucking beautiful day.'
Sarah Miles in *White Mischief*

Rocco: *Fucking . . . what the fuck? Who the fuck fucked this fucking . . . How did you two fucking fucks . . . [shouts] fuck!*
Connor: *Well, that certainly illustrates the diversity of the word.*
Sean Patrick Flanery (as Connor) and David Della Rocco in *The Boondock Saints*

'Fuck damnation, man! Fuck redemption! We are God's unwanted children? So be it!'
Brad Pitt in *Fight Club*

'Phone call for Mike Hunt. Has anyone seen Mike Hunt?'
Kaki Hunter in *Porky's*

'What the fuck are you doing? You're hanging around my fuckin' neck like a vulture, like impending death.'
Joe Pesci in *Goodfellas*

Derivation: 'Bugger'

a) noun – one who commits buggery
b) verb – to commit buggery

'Bugger' can be used as an insult, a general expletive
('bugger it!'), to say that something's gone wrong ('it's
buggered') or to describe a difficult task ('putting that shelf
up was a bugger').

Despite its original meaning, it is generally considered so
mild that many use it as a term of affection in phrases such
as 'you jammy bugger'. In fact, it started as a form of racial
abuse in the fourteenth century and from the Latin
bulgarus made its way through Old French to become
bougre, or 'heretic'. The heretics in question were the
Bogomils, a Christian sect who followed the Greek Church
and a doctrine which was condemned by the rest of the
Church. By the sixteenth century this connotation with
spiritual perversion became allied with what was seen as
sexual perversion, and, ultimately, the word came to mean
'sodomite'. The French word *bougre* became 'bugger' in
Britain, and retained its meaning.

In 1667, the English poet William Chamberlayne blamed
foreign money lenders for the decline of standards in
England, and bemoaned 'the sin of buggery, brought to
England by the Lombards'. (Incidentally, today L.O.M.B.A.R.D.
is an acronym meaning 'Loads of Money But A Right Dick'.)

Part of the 1956 UK Sexual Offences Act refers to buggery, defining it as sexual intercourse between males or between male and female in an 'unnatural manner', or between male or female with an animal in any manner whatsoever.
In the seventeenth century, Lord Rochester, a wit and poet from the court of Charles II, wrote the scandalous lines:

> *But cowards shall forget to rant*
> *Schoolboys to frigg, old whores to paint*
> *The Jesuits fraternity*
> *Shall leave the use of buggery*
> *'A RAMBLE IN SAINT JAMES'S PARKE' (1672)*

Variations include: bugger off, bugger me, buggered, buggered up, bugger all, playing silly buggers, bugger about, bugger someone around

Famous Foul-mouths: Actors Behaving Badly

Superstar actors may lead a charmed life, but that doesn't always mean that they use charming language. With Hollywood films and TV shows now containing more rude words than a navvy's tearoom, it is little wonder that the language of the luvvies is less than pure. Here are a few actors with attitude.

Robert Mitchum

The rugged American actor was famed for his bad-boy image and sought to cultivate it as much as possible. Born in 1917 in Connecticut, Mitchum was a rebel from an early age; after running away from home in his teens he was charged with vagrancy. In the early forties he began to get small film roles and within ten years he was a major superstar, with movies such as *The Night of the Hunter* and *Out of the Past* under his belt. A fifty-year career saw him in films such as *Ryan's Daughter*, *Farewell my Lovely* and *Cape Fear*, and his co-stars included Gregory Peck, Lillian Gish and John Mills.

Not all of his colleagues appreciated his baser qualities, however. As author Bob Thomas reveals in *Golden Boy: The Untold Story of William Holden*, Loretta Young, Mitchum's co-star on *Rachel and the Stranger*, made the mistake of bringing a swear box with her to the set, as she did on every film she worked on. Cast and crew were expected to contribute if they swore and the proceeds went to a home for unwed mothers. A 'hell' cost twenty-five cents, a 'goddamn' fifty cents, and so on.

On one occasion Mitchum, infuriated by his sanctimonious co-star, reached into his pocket and pulled out a handful of notes that he proceeded to stuff in the cup. He then let rip at her with a stream of abuse.

Oliver Reed

'Oliver Reed is God' – Quentin Tarantino
Better known for drinking and carousing than swearing, British actor Oliver Reed could still pick a choice word when he'd had a drink or two. As the ultimate lad, before lad culture was fashionable, he once described his career as 'shafting the girlies and downing the sherbie'.

Born in Wimbledon, southwest London, Oliver was sent away

to boarding school at the age of four. Fourteen schools and a stint of National Service later, Oliver's entry into the acting profession came, appropriately, out of a drinking session in Earl's Court after he'd decided to follow his friends into becoming a film extra.

Following a part in a children's television show, he went on to become one of England's most famous actors, starring in such films as *Women in Love*, *Castaway* and *Oliver!*

Now part of TV legend, his appearances on *Aspel* and *After Dark* – while completely shit-faced – demonstrate what he was capable of. On *Aspel* he arrived on set crumpled, drunk, clutching a jug of orange juice (with gin, it is thought), singing 'Wild Thing'. On the late-night talk-show *After Dark*, he admired a fellow guest's 'tits' before snogging the shocked feminist author Kate Millett.

Always fond of flashing his tackle, he was sacked from the 1995 film *Cutthroat Island* after dropping his trousers at a party to show crew members the tattoo on his penis. Co-star Geena Davis wasn't amused.

In his autobiography *Winner Takes All: A Life Of Sorts*, the director Michael Winner, a friend of the actor, recalls working with Reed and Robert Mitchum on *The Big Sleep*.

> *One day, we were filming at a house in the staid suburb of Chorleywood, Hertfordshire. It was summer. Oliver, Bob Mitchum and I were sitting on the lawn.*
>
> *Oliver suddenly stood up and said, 'You know, Bob, last night I was playing this game where two people have their legs astride a pole and they're naked and they hit at each other to see which one can knock the other off the pole. It completely did in my bollocks. Would you like to see them?'*
>
> *Mitchum said, 'Not really.' I kept silent.*
>
> *Oliver said, 'I'd like to show you.' There were a few members of the public watching us over the low wall of this suburban house. They had the pleasure of seeing Oliver Reed take his trousers down, revealing a very sore genital*

*area. He exposed it closely to Robert Mitchum, although,
thank God, not to me.*

*The residents of Chorleywood took it very well. They kept
watching as if nothing was happening. Oliver then put his
private parts away and resumed the role of perfect gent.*

Colin Farrell

Having launched his American film career shortly after a stint on
the quaint Sunday-night BBC drama *Ballykissangel*, Colin
Farrell took the film industry by storm, in more ways than one.
His screen presence in such movies as *Phone Booth*, *Minority
Report* and *The Recruit* won him much praise and catapulted
him onto the Hollywood A-list. Off-screen, the lad from
Castleknock, near Dublin, shocked his fellow actors with his hard
drinking, womanizing and foul language.

On one occasion he appeared at a press conference in
Toronto, and, he recalled later, 'the first word I said was "fuck".'
When asked whether anyone had advised him to tone his
language down, Colin answered, 'My mother gave me a talk.
"Fuck" is a great word.'

In an interview with magazine *Vanity Fair*, Joel Schumacher,
director of *Tigerland* and *Phone Booth*, recalled an incident at a
Hollywood party he attended with the star.

'I overheard Colin talking to this agent's assistant. Very
attractive. All I heard him say was, "You've never seen an
uncircumcised penis?" And I think you know how that story ends.'

Joel explained away Colin's love of profanity: 'Colin likes "a
good crack", as they say. He's a pub lad . . . It's ordinary among
Irish kids. Every other word is "fuck" and "cunt". It's how they
talk to their mates: "How are ya, ya fuckin' cunt?"'

In another interview Colin himself tells the story of a
modelling job he was sent to at the age of seventeen. He and
several other boys were asked to model underwear. 'First we

modelled boxers and shit like that. Then when we thought we were done, this woman pulls out these G-string fucking things and says, "Any volunteers?"' The interviewer asked if he took the opportunity and Colin replies, 'You bet. Fuck, man. It was ten extra pounds! That was a fucking hit of E right there. I was seventeen fucking years old. I did it. I modelled the fucking red G-string on telly, with the slit crawling up my bare ass . . . '

When an American magazine named him as the world's most profane celebrity, the caption below his picture read 'Fucking hell! I won a fucking award!'

John Malkovich

The actor from Illinois and star of such films as *Dangerous Liaisons, In the Line of Fire* and *The Killing Fields* often tells a story about being in the first grade and losing an Easter-egg contest. Apparently he called the teacher a 'motherfucker' ('or "cocksucker", I can't remember which') and walked out of the school. He remembers his father 'beat my ass for about six hours'.

In an interview in *Entertainment Weekly* in 1993, Malkovich talked of his worries about the violence society exposes children to, before admitting that he took his own two children to see the brutal gangland film *Menace II Society*. He recounts a story about his son Loewy, then aged one: 'Of course, my little boy did say the other day, when I made him get off the dining room table, "Fuck you, Dada" very clearly.'

He also revealed that, like his dad, Loewy is a fan of Dr Dre, and that his first complete sentence was 'More Dr Dre'.

Ewan McGregor

The down-to-earth Scot who became an international superstar in films such as *Trainspotting, Moulin Rouge* and the *Star*

Wars series maintains the use of a certain amount of his 'native' language. The son of two teachers, and born in Crieff, Perthshire, McGregor proved his love of profanity while making a documentary of his journey around the world on a motorbike with a friend. In *The Long Way Round*, Ewan and friend Charlie Boorman effed and blinded their way through several continents. As a review of the accompanying book (from *Realclassic.co.uk*) puts it, 'nearly every utterance in the book is well peppered with the F-word.' It continues, 'There was little, if any, soliloquizing, philosophical thoughts . . . in one three-line paragraph they manage the F-word four times! And the reader is given the impression that these young men have had an education and might know a few other adjectives to describe their situations.'

In recent interview in *The Daily Telegraph*, McGregor comments that he doesn't just enjoy riding motorbikes; he 'fucking' loves it. And that his career and lifestyle make him 'one lucky cunt'.

A former hellraiser who has calmed down, got married, had two children and given up drinking and smoking, he still indulges his swearing habit. While admitting his job is 'heady and glamorous and fucking fantastic,' his family come first: 'It affords us a very comfortable life. But none of it would mean a single fucking thing if I didn't have them to share it with.'

In another interview, in *Details* magazine, he admits his mouth used to get him into trouble as a lad and recalls one memorable occasion on a golf course:

'We use to play a lot on public courses, just for something to do. When I was fourteen, I got thrown off a golf course for swearing. After every shot I would get really angry, screaming, "Fuck! Cunt! Fucking Cunt!"

'Eventually this guy drove up in a tractor and told me I had to leave because the other golfers had been complaining. So I had to walk back in shame with my clubs. I didn't play for a long time after that.'

Derivation: 'Bitch'

a) noun – a female dog, wolf, fox or otter
b) noun – an dislikeable or spiteful person, usually a woman
c) noun – a person under another's control, 'he's my bitch'
d) verb – to complain
e) adjective – to be unpleasant, as in, 'she's so bitchy'

'Bitch' has an historic pedigree among British swear words, a variety of uses, and has graced centuries of verbal abuse. Heralding from the Old English *bicce*, from the Old Norse *bikkja*, referring to the female dog (and similar mammals), 'bitch' in this sense first appeared circa AD 1000. *A Dictionary of Vulgar Terms* illustrates a usage more familiar to modern readers, stating it to be a 'most offensive appellation that can be given to an English woman, even more provoking than that of "whore"'.

While still used in its original sense by dog breeders, the original meaning of 'bitch' has widened considerably. The verb 'to bitch' means to grumble about something excessively, as well as to make another subserviant to your control – they are then 'your bitch' (a term often used in prisons between male convicts). The familiar adjective 'bitchy' is common and needs no explanation. A less familiar usage of 'bitch' as a noun refers to the poor sod sat in the middle seat of a truck – so called because they have the least room to move. And, of course, the MTV generation will recognize the alternative pronunciation and spelling 'biatch', which reflects how the word is spoken in rap and hip-hop music.

Variations include: bitchin', (a) bitch slap, bitch-fest, riding bitch

Lyrical Language

Although music has always served as a way for people to express themselves, it is only comparatively recently that swearing on records has caused such controversy – or perhaps that's because it is only recently that such an avalanche of abuse has hit our high-street music stores?

The censorship of music in the fifties and sixties, in both the UK and America, was usually due to a work's theme or subject matter rather than actual profanity content. In 1956, for example, Billie Holiday's haunting song 'Love For Sale' was banned in the States because it was clearly about a prostitute, while Cole Porter's 'I Get A Kick Out Of You' was banned from the airwaves because of the line 'I get no kick from cocaine' – later, in 1962, Sinatra sang the line as 'Some like the perfume from Spain.' In 1964, the governor of Indiana, Matthew Welsh, asked the State Broadcasters' Association to ban the song 'Louie, Louie' by The Kingsmen because he considered it to be pornographic. In 1970, John Lennon rocked the boat with his 'Working Class Hero' because it contained the F-word (as a result of which it was banned). But, despite these incidents, it wasn't until the advent of punk in the mid-seventies that vinyl vituperation began to cause a regular problem for the broadcasters.

The famous banning of Frankie Goes to Hollywood's 'Relax' in 1983 was a turning point in the censorship of records on the radio, although the current policy at Radio One, the essential station for artists who hope to make it into the charts, is that no record is ever banned.

'We play hip-hop records all the time but, during the day, we play radio-edit versions which are agreed between us and the record company,' explains a spokesman for Radio One. 'There is no watershed as such, but anything with bad language in it may be played late at night.'

In both the UK and the US there is no law against recording and selling such records, however, in the States for example, the FCC can fine radio stations that play records it considers 'indecent', prompting Eminem's line 'the FCC won't let me be' in 'Without Me'.

In a 2004 interview, the then British Home Secretary, David Blunkett, responding to the huge rise in hip-hop artists using swear words and references to violent crime, said: 'I am concerned that we need to talk to the record producers, to the distributors, to those who are actually engaged in the music business about what is and isn't acceptable.' However, in a country that regards civil liberties and freedom of speech as sacred, his call for censorship is unlikely to gain much support from the public.

Don't Ban it, Sticker it

The Parental Advisory Sticker was introduced in 1990 to show parents more clearly which records contain lyrics that may be unsuitable for children. The original idea came from Tipper Gore, the wife of American politician Al Gore. After buying a Prince album for her twelve-year-old daughter, she was shocked to discover that some of the lyrics were overtly sexual (d'oh!). She sprung into action and set up the pressure group 'Parents' Music Resource Group'. The music industry was forced to give in and the black, so-called 'Tipper sticker' was born.

Of course, the sticker often has exactly the opposite effect to that Tipper intended. As anyone who rushed out to buy Frankie Goes to Hollywood's 'Relax' or giggled with their pals over the lyrics of 'Friggin' in the Riggin'' could testify, the stickers merely make the records more desirable in the eyes of adolescents.

Advisory stickers are currently fixed to about 1 per cent of CDs where record companies consider them to contain sexually explicit, violent or offensive content. Artists who have been 'stickered' include Eminem, The Beautiful South and Dr Dre.

Here are some singles (and singers) that have fallen foul of the foul-language police.

Bob Dylan – In 1968, a radio station in El Paso, Texas, banned all records by Dylan because they found it too difficult to make out the lyrics. The station management, not understanding what was being said, thought it would err on the side of caution just in case Dylan was singing anything lewd or obscene.

John Lennon was never one to respect authority and he proved it, yet again, with his searing take on societal repression and poverty in 'Working Class Hero' (1970), which includes the lines:

They hate you if you're clever and they despise a fool
'Til you're so fucking crazy you can't follow their rules

. . . .

And you think you're so clever and classless and free
But you're still fucking peasants as far as I can see

Ian Dury and the Blockheads released 'F**king Ada' in 1980, but not surpisingly it failed to make the Radio One playlist. The chorus consists of the words 'Fucking Ada', repeated four times. In total the offending line is repeated forty-eight times.

Unsurprisingly, **The Dead Kennedys**' 1981 party anthem 'Too Drunk To Fuck' failed to make it past the censors and on to the radio, but that didn't stop every schoolboy in the country rushing out to buy a copy. After drinking sixteen beers, the 'hero' of the song starts a fight, and then suffers from consuming so much:

But now I'm jaded
You're out of luck
I'm rollin' down the stairs
Too drunk to fuck

Another verse reads:

You give me head
It makes it worse
Take out your fuckin' retainer
Put it in your purse

Neil Young's 1990 composition 'Fucking Up' was also banned, for obvious reasons. The title is repeated in the chorus when the veteran musician asks himself the eternal question, 'Why do I keep fuckin' up?'

Super Furry Animals – Funnily enough, the BBC thought that the Welsh band Super Furry Animals were less than cuddly when they released their 1996 single 'The Man Don't Give a Fuck'. As well as the title (blunt and to the point!), the song contains over fifty occurrences of the F-word.

'Fatboy Slim is Fucking in Heaven' manages to combine numerous repetition (108 times) of a rude word with blasphemy – two offences for the price of one! Such a high swear-count is remarkable until it's realized that the song's entire lyric is a repetition of the title phrase (or parts of the title phrase).

Going for several minutes, the genius wordsmith (excuse my sarcasm) eventually seems to come to his senses and ends with the disclaimer, 'All right, please don't play this for anybody. I don't normally do this.' Seems the BBC chose to comply with his request and the record stayed off the airwaves.

The Rolling Stones changed the name of their 1973 song 'Star fucker' to 'Star Star', but that was not quite enough to appease the folks of the broadcasting world. The song, a tribute to the band's more devoted groupies, repeated the phrase 'Star fucker' over and over again in the chorus, and contained several graphic sexual references. The chorus goes:

Yeah! You're a star fucker, star fucker, star fucker,
  star fucker, star
Yeah, a star fucker, star fucker, star fucker, star fucker, star
A star fucker, star fucker, star fucker, star fucker, star

A later verse conveys the hedonistic and frankly pornographic acts that it is assumed most rock stars get up to. First there's the indecent photos, and then Mick shares with us how the star fucker's 'trick with fruit was kinda cute / I bet you keep your pussy clean'. Rock and roll! Another verse contains the lines:

Ali MacGraw got mad with you
For givin' head to Steve McQueen

Linda McCartney seems an unlikely candidate to incur the wrath of the straight-laced brigade, but she is (probably) the only artist to be banned for swearing *after* her death. Radio and TV stations angered Sir Paul McCartney when they refused to play the 1999 single 'The Light Comes From Within', which contains the line:

You say I'm simple, you say I'm a hick
You're fucking no one, you stupid dick

Sir Paul claimed that the song, a reply to those critics who had slammed Linda as untalented and mocked her belief in animal rights, had been 'universally banned' and that *Top of the Pops*, *Live and Kicking* and various BBC radio stations had refused to add the single to their playlist. In response, Sir Paul launched a campaign to 'let parents decide', taking out adverts in a number of national newspapers asking parents to consider whether children would be 'morally corrupted' by the controversial lyrics.

The BBC denied there was a blanket ban though, and said that they would play an edited version. Outspoken Radio One DJ Chris Moyles, however, pulled no punches when he revealed the real reason for the ban, telling listeners: 'It's a poor lyric. I can't remember the last time we played a Linda McCartney record – or Paul McCartney come to think of it. If it's not good enough to get on the Radio One playlist, end of story, forget who it is.

'I feel sorry for Paul, and I was upset when Linda died, but these are stupid lyrics and we can't play it for that reason alone.'

Tune In, Tone Down

While trying to dodge the censors may be fun for mischievous music-makers, clearly being refused airplay can sometimes be detrimental to record sales. Several artists have found ways around a ban by toning down their language for the radio edit.

Radiohead's first big hit 'Creep', released in 1992, contained the line, 'I wish I was special. You're so fucking special.' In order to get it played on the radio the lyrics were changed to 'You're so very special.'

The Beautiful South's 1996 anti-marriage anthem 'Don't Marry Her, Have Me', started life as 'Don't Marry Her, Fuck Me', and contained the same explicit line in the chorus. For radio purposes the lyrics were changed, but they remained the same on the album, which was, of course, stickered. Despite the radio edit, the song still contained the wonderful euphemism, 'She'll grab your Sandra Bullocks and slowly raise her knee.'

Prince's sleazy 1992 number 'Sexy Motherfucker' was renamed 'Sexy MF', but was banned from all UK radio stations anyway. It still reached number four in the charts.

The Stranglers – Concept album *Men in Black*'s 1997 single 'Peaches' contained the line, 'Oh shit, there goes the charabanc. Look's like I'm going to be stuck here all summer. What a bummer.' Although 'shit' was removed for the radio version, 'bummer' was allowed to stay in. Another line that had to be changed was, 'Is she trying to get out of that clitoris? Liberation for women, that's what I preach.' The word 'clitoris' was changed to 'bikini' and the song reached the top ten in the UK.

Incidentally, many of the websites listing Stranglers' lyrics, which tend to be set up by male fans, have the aforementioned line as 'Is she trying to get out of that clitares?', proving once and for all that most men can't find the clitoris – even in the dictionary!

The Lemonheads took the humorous approach to censorship when changing the lyrics of 'Big Gay Heart'. They spoonerized 'suck my dick' to 'duck my sick' for radio play, and changed 'piss me off' to 'tick me off'.

Puff Daddy's somewhat antagonistic 'Come With Me' (with Jimmy Page) includes several uses of the F-word:

Fuck my enemies
Fuck my foes

. . . .

I want to fight you
I'll fucking bite you

The offending words were deleted for the single versions although, bizarrely, the Japanese import had Godzilla roaring over the rude bits!

The American band, **MC5** (originally called Motor City Five), caused a huge stir with their track 'Kick Out the Jams', which contained the first recorded use of 'motherfucker' in a song. It was banned from innumerable radio stations and high-school dances as well as the US chain store, Hudson's. Not to be beaten, the rebellious band took out a full-page adverts saying 'FUCK HUDSON'S' in the underground press. The stunt backfired somewhat when MC5 were dropped by their record company as a result of the controversy.

The Sex Pistols, comprising of Johnny Rotten, Steve Jones, Paul Cook and Glen Matlock, were fond of causing havoc and famously swore on live TV (see page 33). Their 1977 single 'God Save the Queen' reached number two in the charts, despite being banned as unpatriotic. Furthermore, on the B-side of the 1979 single 'Something Else' was the filthy song 'Friggin' in the Riggin", which contained the lines:

It was on the good ship Venus,
By Christ you should have seen us
The figurehead was a whore in bed
And the mast a mammoth penis

More controversy came when the lads released their LP, charmingly entitled *Never Mind the Bollocks*. In order to prevent the album title from being censored, the Sex Pistols became embroiled in a court case during which their lawyer explained that the derivation of the word 'bollocks' is probably not a rude one, but refers to a pulley-block at the head of a topmast, otherwise known as a 'bullock block' (and which was of course what the band had in mind all along!). The judge believed this cock-and-bull story and ruled that 'bollocks' was not a swear word.

The Eurythmics' 1984 hit 'Sexcrime (1984)' was banned by several US radio stations because of its repeated use of the unforgivable words 'sex' and 'crime'.

Pink's 2003 single 'Like a Pill' contained the reasonably mild line 'She's being a little bitch', which was deemed fine for radio but was altered, understandably, for a live performance on kids' TV show *CD:UK*, to 'witch'. However, the fact that Pink sang the song wearing a T-shirt which read 'You fucking bitch' was somehow overlooked. LWT were forced to apologize.

In April 2004, at the age of twenty-one, **Eamon** rocked the charts in both the UK and the US when he leapt to number one with song about the breakdown of a relationship. 'Fuck It [I Don't Want You Back]' contained no less than thirty-three expletives including a chorus which went:

Fuck what I said, it don't mean shit now

. . . .

Fuck you, you hoe, I don't want you back

The single sold almost 550,000 copies in the UK and earned the young singer from New York the dubious title of 'King Of The F-word'. The record company originally wanted Eamon, full name Eamon Doyle, to change the lyrics and title to 'Forget It', but he refused and in the process became an overnight sensation across the world. Shocked journalists and broadcasters called for the record to be censored and a huge debate broke out. Eamon, who insists the song is about the hurt caused by a specific break-up and is not a general diatribe against women commented, 'It amazes me that there's been a fuss over me cursing when there's rappers talking about killing people.' Perhaps he has a point.

Soon after the success of the record, a singer claiming to be the ex-girlfriend to whom 'Fuck It' referred launched a counterattack. Frankee reached number one with 'F.U.R.B. (FU Right Back)', but Eamon is adamant that he has never met her.

The Rappers' Delight

The last two decades have seen a rise in the popularity of hip-hop and rap music, and particularly of the subgenre known as gangsta rap. Portraying the culture of inner-city gangs, street life and violence, gangsta rap is renowned for its aggressive, no-holds-barred lyrics, gritty themes and often questionable attitudes to women – as well as, naturally, a great deal of swearing. 'Fuck', 'motherfucker' and 'ass' are commonplace, as are most other profanities you can think of. Two infamous paragons of joyful gangsta-rap swearing are given below.

Eminem

The most successful white rapper on the scene, Eminem has had huge success with records such as 'The Way I Am' and 'My Name Is'. Perhaps his most famous song, however, is 'Stan', the story of an obsessed Eminem fan who commits suicide by driving off a bridge, killing his girlfriend and her unborn child in the process. The letter that 'Stan' writes to Eminem start like most fan letters – acknowledging his allegiance to the idol, and how much he respects the musician. But the subsequent verses reveal a darker undercurrent, until 'Stan' begins to berate the star for neglecting to respond; in particular, after a show.

> *But you coulda signed an autograph for Matthew*
> *That's my little brother man, he's only six years old*
> *We waited in the blistering cold for you for hours and*
> *   you just said, 'No.'*
> *That's pretty shitty man – you're like his fuckin' idol*

On another track, 'The Real Slim Shady', he attacks Will Smith for the clean language of his records.

> *Will Smith don't gotta cuss in his raps to sell his records*
> *Well I do, so fuck him and fuck you too!*

Just to prove the point, in a collaborative track with US performer Kid Rock – called, appropriately, 'Fuck Off' – he has the following to say:

> *It's 1998 and you still can't fuck with me*
> *You don't be fuckin' with the blue eye*
> *Fuckin' with my 2-5 up your fuckin' ass like my shoe size*
>
> . . . .
>
> *So fuck off*

Dr Dre

Formerly a member of NWA (Niggaz with Attitude), Dr Dre is no feminist's friend. His graphic lyrics contain frequent and disturbing references to the subjugation of women and to sexual acts. By way of example, the charmingly entitled 'Fuck You' starts with a loving answer-machine message from a woman who keeps saying 'I love you'. Her affection is answered with a stream of abusive sexual imagery as Dr Dre raps:

> *I just wanna fuck bad bitches*
> *All them nights I never had bitches*
> *Now I'm all up in that ass bitches*

His collaborator Snoop Dogg adds:

> *So whatcha gon' do, ya freak bitch?*
> *You actin' like you don't do dicks*
>
> . . . .
>
> *So I gave her some Hennesey, she gave me some head*
> *I fucked her on the flo', so I wouldn't mess up my bed*

Perhaps not unsurprisingly, it isn't only women that Dr Dre has offended. In 1990, he and the other members of NWA received a letter from the FBI that stated the agency did not appreciate the song 'Fuck The Police'. Law-enforcement groups across the US were in firm agreement (can't imagine why!).

Derivation: 'Crap'

a) noun – excrement or something that is rubbish
b) verb – to pass excrement
c) adjective – as in 'this is a crap film'

'Crap' is a less vulgar version of 'shit' and is used in much the same way. It can either refer to the bodily function, as in 'I need to take a crap', or to something that is not very good, i.e. 'this is crap'. The popular theory on the origin of the word is that it derives from the name of famous Victorian plumber Thomas Crapper, but his influence on the development of the toilet we know today has been much exaggerated – rather, he worked on several developments which, along with those by other inventors, contributed to the flushing toilet. However, Crapper's name does appear on manhole covers in Westminster Abbey.

Unfortunately for school kids across the land, he did not inspire the word 'crap'. The word seems to have been used in the late eighteenth century, fifty years before the snigger-inspiring inventor was born.

One possible explanation is that it is linked to the Middle English *crappe* meaning 'chaff' or other waste residue, and perhaps also the Latin *crappa*, which meant the same. The first reference to crap as a verb is in 1846, but this was US usage, not British. The cockney rhyming slang version of the word is 'pony', as in 'pony and trap'.

Variations include: crappy, crapping, crapping myself

Famous Foul-mouths: Sporty but Naughty

The locker room has traditionally been a place of cursing, swearing and general ribaldry, and lads getting together to play a sport is bound to result in a little blue banter. One or two on the following list, however, have brought their bad language on to the pitch, and that's just not cricket.

Mike Gatting

The English cricket captain became a sporting legend when he sparked an international incident by calling an umpire a 'bastard'.

The event was a Test Match against Pakistan in Faisalabad in December 1987. The England team, already tired from a gruelling World Cup tour, had just played Pakistan in Lahore where the umpiring had been criticized for the numerous dodgy decisions against the England team. Gatting himself was the victim of dubious leg-before-wicket decision, which made him so angry he ran two laps of the Gadaffi stadium to calm himself down.

After a dubious though vociferous accusation of 'cheating' by Shakoor Rana (in his actual words Gatting was 'a fucking cheating cunt'), the square-leg umpire, Gatting defended his actions, only to hear Rana walk away uttering a few choice words of his own. Gatting finally lost the plot and squared up to the umpire, pointing his finger and calling him a 'bastard'.

The game was stopped and Shakoor Rana demanded a public apology, refusing to start the third day's play until he got one. Gatting said he deserved an apology for being called a cheat. The Pakistan and England Cricket Boards intervened and, eventually, Mike Gatting apologized. The incident made headlines all over the world and sparked an international debate in which even the Foreign Office became involved.

Shakoor Rana, who sadly has passed away since the incident, was quoted at the time as saying: 'Calling me a bastard may be excusable in England, but here people murder someone who calls another man a bastard.'

Gatting has since admitted it wasn't his best cricketing memory. 'It wasn't a very proud moment of my career. It is one of those things that has gone down in history. It will probably always be remembered.'

John McEnroe

Clive James once remarked, 'McEnroe was charming as always. Which means that he was as charming as a dead mouse in a loaf of bread.'

The legendary Wimbledon champion is as famous for his temper as his tennis and, at the height of his career, he caused regular controversy with his abuse of umpires and crowds. McEnroe gained world renown when he halted Bjorn Borg's run of Wimbledon titles by beating him in the final of the Men's Singles in 1981. But, during his first match of the tournament, he directed a stream of abuse at umpire Ted James, calling him 'the pits of the world', before swearing at tournament referee Fred Hoyles. He was fined $1,500 and earned the title of 'Superbrat'.

He went on to win seven Grand Slam singles titles, including three Wimbledon wins (1981, 1983 and 1984) – all accompanied by a catalogue of outbursts, swear words, insults and fines.

In 1987 he took a seven-month break from the game after playing at the US Open, at which he was fined $17,500 and suspended for two months for misconduct and verbal abuse.

At the 1990 Australian Open in Melbourne against Swede Mikael Pernfors, McEnroe was issued a warning for intimidating a lineswoman and then docked a point for smashing a racquet. Clearly annoyed, he told the tournament supervisor Ken Farrar to 'just go fuck your mother'. British umpire Gerry Armstrong promptly announced: 'Verbal abuse, audible obscenity, Mr McEnroe. Default. Game, set and match, Pernfors.'

Novelist and tennis writer Michael Mewshaw tells a story of a journalist friend who found himself in the gents with McEnroe at Wimbledon. The journalist approached his hero and said, 'Hi, John, I'm Sal Palantonio of ESPN.' 'Fuck you,' McEnroe responded, 'and fuck ESPN.'

Washington Post journalist Barry Lorge said, 'He came across as a precocious brat – immensely talented, spoiled and rather obnoxious. On the court, he pouted, cursed, threw his racket . . .

Derivation: 'Motherfucker'

In recent years, largely due to the influence of Hollywood films, the word 'motherfucker' has spread from the United States to the shores of the UK. Commonly thought to have originated in African-American communities, it became a popular insult during the Vietnam War and spread with the return of the troops. It is widely thought that the term refers to someone base enough to sleep with their own mother, but this is a misconception. In fact, the term 'motherfucker' was first coined by African slaves and referred to the slave owners who raped the slaves' mothers. In some communities it is used as an affectionate term, much as the British use 'bastard' (as in 'you lucky motherfucker') and it is often abbreviated to become, simply, 'mother'. I'm not sure the respectable ladies of the Mothers' Union would approve.

Variations include: motherfucking, mothering, mother-humping

He was a cry baby. Off-court, he demonstrated little savoir-faire.'

Even his own father, John Snr, admitted he gobs off a bit. 'John sets high standards for himself and doesn't suffer fools gladly,' he said. 'What you might say about John is that he shoots from the hip through his mouth.'

In a 2003 interview with the magazine *Maxim*, just before McEnroe had started his own chat show in the US (which bombed dismally), he was asked if he had mellowed. It seemed he hadn't.

'Today really set me off!' he told the journalist. 'Tell me: why the fuck was there a goddamn desk on the court for this photo shoot when they're not even letting me have a desk on the goddamn show? It's fucking absurd!'

When asked how the anger management was going 'Mac' replied, 'I still get frustrated on a daily basis. I grew up in an Irish-American family where that was normal. My parents would be screaming, "Goddamn it, you asshole . . . I love you!" That's why I love New York. You're lucky if you go ten minutes without somebody calling you an asshole driving in from the airport.'

Now retired from professional tennis, McEnroe makes money from commentating and the occasional appearance on court where, he jokingly claims, 10 per cent of his fee is docked if he *doesn't* swear or break a racquet: 'I used to get fined if I cursed and now I get fined if I don't.'

On a BBC website recently, McEnroe said that anger helped him on the court: 'Before I had kids it definitely helped. After I had kids I started to question whether it would come back to be a poor example and tougher to explain. If it's done in the right way, if you're not swearing for example and just letting out some excess energy, it can be helpful.'

Tim Henman

The British tennis player whose kit (according to the washing-powder ads) – and language – was always whiter than white, shocked the nation at Wimbledon in 2005 when he proved that he, too, knew a few four-letter words. In a memorable game in which he lost to the world No. 152 Dmitry Tursunov, Henman issued a volley of abuse in the first set after the fans, usually inspired into a frenzy of 'Henmania' by the mere mention of his name, stayed curiously quiet.

'Come on,' fumed the angry player. 'Come on, fuck, more! Make some fucking noise! It's fucking unbelievable!'

After that little outburst he turned his frustration on the

ballboys and girls who, apparently, brought him the wrong drink.

'Get them to get their heads out of their arses and get me a Diet Coke out here!'

To make matters worse, the whole thing went out on a live broadcast in the middle of the afternoon. After his second-set defeat, a chastened Tim was sorry for his lapse.

'If I have said some bad words, I apologize,' he said. 'These things happen on the spur of the moment when you are out there competing and wanting to get fired up.'

A BBC spokesman said, 'The swearing was broadcast live and the BBC would like to apologize for any offence caused. It is one of the dangers of broadcasting a major live sporting event, but it is live coverage the viewers want to see.'

So, evidently, did the newspapers. The swearing got as much coverage in the nationals as the game itself!

Roy Keane

In 2002, as the Republic of Ireland prepared for the World Cup that was to be held in Japan and Korea, a row broke out between manager Mick McCarthy and fiery captain Roy Keane.

Manchester United star Roy thought that the preparations for the World Cup weren't up to standard and that the facilities on the island of Saipon were poor. The training pitch was inadequate, which cut down training time, the hotel was substandard, and some of the kit and equipment arrived late. Keane blamed manager Mick McCarthy and felt that the lack of professionalism was damaging the team's chances.

When he confronted McCarthy, the manager asked him about an ankle injury and, according to Keane, accused him of faking an injury and not supporting his teammates. At the final showdown, Roy allegedly told Mick: 'You were a crap player and you are a crap manager. The only reason I have any dealings with you is that somehow you are the manager of my country and you're not

Derivation: 'Git'

a) noun – a contemptible person

Considered a very mild term of abuse in modern day society, its original meaning was similar to that of 'bastard' – an illegitimate person. It takes its origin from the archaic verb 'to beget' meaning to create something, or to bring into the world a child, so your 'get' therefore meant your brood, and particularly illegitimate offspring. 'Get' is still used in parts of northwest England and Scotland instead of the word 'git'.

'Git' does *not* mean a pregnant camel, as anyone who was at primary school in the seventies and eighties may well believe. If you remember retorting to the abuse with the phrase 'I'm not a pregnant camel', you will be sorry to learn that that particular rumour, apparently started in West Lodge Middle School in Pinner, Middlesex, was completely false.

even Irish, you English cunt. You can stick it up your bollocks . . . you were a cunt in 1994, again in 1998 and you're even more of a cunt now – and you ain't even Irish.'

The outburst got Roy Keane stripped of his captaincy and sent home on the next plane. At a radio interview shortly afterwards, he was challenged about the language by Irish journalist Tommie Gorman, who said he was not setting a good example to children.

'It was a private meeting amongst men,' answered an

unrepentant Roy. 'These things aren't supposed to go out. That's why I went to Mick's room on the Sunday night and I discussed with it with him. Mick was the one who called it in front of everyone else and said I'd turned my back on the players, that I faked a injury not to go off to Iran when he knew damn well I wasn't right. And he's supposed to be a man-manager. So of course there was going to be language. I wasn't going to say, "Excuse me Mick, I think you're a bit out of order." Of course you're going to use language. I said things to Mick and I'm 100 per cent behind what I said.'

In the same World Cup tournament Slovenian player Zlatko Zahovic was also sent home after telling his manager, 'I can buy you, your house, and your family. You were a dickhead player and you're the same as a coach.'

Was there something in the water?

Wayne Rooney

Liverpudlian superstar Wayne Rooney grew up wanting to play for Everton and, by the age of sixteen, had a place in his beloved team. He went on to become the youngest player to play, and score, for England and, in 2004, left his home team to become a star striker at Manchester United. In Euro 2004 he became England's top scorer, despite breaking his foot in a game against Portugal and, by the time he was nineteen, was already recognized as one of the most talented players of all time.

However his temper, both on and off the pitch, has ensured that he is rarely out of the headlines and his language, particularly during matches, has got him into trouble.

The most memorable incident was a match between Manchester United and Arsenal in February 2005. Wayne was caught on camera directing a torrent of obscenities at the referee

Graham Poll. It was estimated that over a hundred swear words were uttered by the teenage player during the match, and at one point the swear count was up to twenty words a minute. He had already been booked for dissent when he unleashed his tirade against Poll. The referee, rather than sending him off, called captain Roy Keane (who had earlier been caught on camera giving Arsenal's Patrick Vieira a similarly abusive tongue-lashing in the players' tunnel) to calm him down. This he did, but the incident wasn't quite over yet. Everyone became involved in the issue of swearing and football, partly because such tirades could be witnessed by young children.

'Young people behaving like Wayne Rooney does on the football pitch are increasingly finding themselves in front of an exclusions panel,' claimed Dr Chris Howard, a head teacher from South Wales, who is a leading member of the National Association for Head Teachers.

'He's an eighteen-year-old role model for millions,' said Dr Howard. 'But he sets a bad example. Rooney used a tirade of four-letter words – and yet he stayed on the pitch . . . Children see Rooney getting away with yobbish behaviour and believe they can do the same themselves.'

As a result of the incident, as well as one or two lurid stories in the tabloids, Rooney was reportedly asked to stay away from a children's football tournament where he was due to coach an under-thirteens' team because the organizers and sponsors (Coca-Cola) didn't think he was a suitable role model.

Still, his granny continues to think he's an angel. In a letter to the *Liverpool Echo*, published in May 2005, Pat Morrey defended her grandson and said that the media were 'picking on' poor Wayne. Urging people to see his good side she wrote, 'Wayne isn't as bad as people make out. He never swears in front of his family.'

Graham Taylor

The former manager of Watford and Aston Villa became the England manager in 1990, shortly after Bobby Robson had got the national team as far as the semi-finals in the World Cup. But Graham was not destined to lead the team further and, in November 1993, he resigned after England failed to qualify for the 1994 World Cup.

Not unusually for football managers, Graham was partial to the odd swear word, particularly when the lads weren't performing as well as they should. But in Graham's case, the language of the locker room was caught on camera when he agreed to do a *Cutting Edge* documentary about his life as England's manager. *Graham Taylor: An Impossible Job* was broadcast on Channel Four in 1994 and contained a total of twenty-seven 'fucks'.

Ten years later, in an interview with *The Guardian* newspaper, he defended the shocking documentary. 'The thing was the programme was made over eighteen months and during that time I must have said the F-word twenty-seven times, and every single one was left in,' he said. 'I don't think twenty-seven F-words over the course of eighteen months is bad by professional football standards.'

'It might sound hard to believe, but since I've left football I hardly swear at all,' Graham went on. 'Football's an environment where saying, "Please No. 10, would you mind kindly marking that player?" doesn't really work. You have to put some language in. Swearing emphasizes what you want them to do and they seem to understand that. That's how it is and I think a lot of people at that time knew that. But I was the villain, and I was never going to get any plaudits for it.'

Griff Sanders

The name may not be familiar, but Griff Sanders is a legend in his own sport as the bad boy of . . . err . . . bowling. The Lawn Bowling champion was an England International at twenty-five, when he was banned from outdoor lawn bowls events for swearing, inappropriate dress and using obscene language towards an official. Other misdemeanours included drinking lager and rolling cigarettes on the green, and playing a game while eating a bag of chips, as well as writing insulting comments about a club secretary on his score card.

The Devon County Bowling Association were so appalled by his behaviour that they banned him for ten years in 1998, but Griff was having none of it. He appealed against the ban and, a year later, it was overturned.

Griff defended his use of 'excessive swearing' on the pitch: 'I swear a bit sometimes and offend people, but I would never humiliate anyone on the green. I just get angry with myself really – I just can't help showing my emotions, that's all.'

Griff became a legend outside of the bowls set after Paul Kaye played a character based on him in the 2003 movie *Blackball*, directed by Mel Smith.

Filthy
Wordplay

Wordplay is always a joy,

especially when the words

involved are filthy.

The Ones That Got Away; Or, Swear Words No Longer With Us

'Swive'

In medieval times the word 'fuck' didn't exist; instead, the common profanity meaning 'to copulate' was 'swive'. Although like 'fuck' its use was flexible, 'swive' didn't have quite the range of our more modern invective – 'swive' was never used as an adjective, as in, 'will you pass me the swiving salt!', nor a verb ('swive off!'). According to the *Oxford English Dictionary*, 'Don't bathe on a full stomach, nor swive' was advice given in 1440. Chaucer used the expression in 'The Miller's Tale' when explaining the conclusion of a love triangle:

> *Thus swyved was this carpenteris wyf*
> *For al his kepyng and his jalousye*
> *And Absolon hath kist hir nether ye.*

Unfortunately, by the late nineteenth century, the word had all but disappeared.

'Quim'

A seventeenth- and eighteenth-century word for the female sexual organs. Possibly related to the obsolete word 'queme', meaning 'pleasant'.

'Zounds'

The Parliamentary Act titled 'To Restrain Abuses of Players' passed in 1606 banned blasphemy from the stage and led to a growth in the number of 'minced oaths'; phrases shortened from the more offensive blasphemies. 'Zounds' became a popular contraction of 'God's wounds'. Originally pronounced to rhyme with 'wounds', within a century it came to be enunciated to rhyme with 'sounds', thereby obscuring its original meaning altogether.

The Ones You Thought You Could Get Away With; Or, The Seemingly Innocent Words With a Less Than Innocent Origin

'Berk'
While most people would think nothing of calling their boss, husband or even their child a 'berk', the origin of the word is anything but innocent. It is, in fact, rhyming slang; the full term being 'Berkshire Hunt' or 'Berkeley Hunt'. Need I say more?

'Cobblers'
Although it is often considered a general expletive, 'cobblers' is actually a reference to the testicles, and comes from the rhyming slang 'Cobbler's awls', meaning 'balls'.

'Pillock'
A favourite term of abuse of Alf Garnett, in *Till Death Us Do Part*, 'pillock' started life as 'pillicock', which is northern English slang for 'penis'. Nowadays the word is considered so mild that hardly an eyelid was batted when British politician Mo Mowlam was filmed during the 2001 general election campaign telling someone that they looked 'a complete pillock' in their shop uniform. Imagine if she'd told them they looked 'a complete prick'!

'Bumf / Bumph'
Commonly used in offices and homes around the country to mean 'useless or excessive paperwork', even your granny wouldn't find this one offensive. Or would she?

In fact, it is a shortened version of the appropriate term 'bum fodder'. Its origin is possibly English school slang and derives from the practice of using unwanted reading material as toilet paper. The full term first appeared in 1653, in Sir Thomas Urquhart's translation of the works of Rabelais.

'Poppycock'

Often thought of as an old-fashioned and stuffy equivalent of the more modern day 'bullshit', the origins of the two words are surprisingly similar. The word derives from the low Dutch expression 'pappa kak' meaning, literally, 'soft shit'.

'Raspberry'

All children love to blow a 'raspberry', and fans of *The Two Ronnies* may remember the classic sketches involving 'The Phantom Raspberry Blower of Old London Town'. Of course a 'raspberry' is merely a rude sound made with the mouth. Or is it? In fact this, too, comes from the rhyming slang for 'fart', i.e. 'raspberry tart'.

'Getting on my wick'

So, you are in polite society and feel it necessary to refrain from using the rather more visual term 'getting on my tits'. What do you do? Substitute it with 'getting on my wick', which, obviously, nobody minds. That's because most people never give the real meaning a second thought. The term actually comes from the rhyming slang for 'prick' or 'dick' – 'Hampton wick' – and it has nothing to do with candles!

'Brass monkeys'

Freezing weather is often said to be 'brass monkeys' or, to use the full phrase, 'cold enough to freeze the balls off a brass monkey'. The term was first recorded in the US in 1857, and there are two or three theories regarding its origin. One story has it that the

Royal Navy's vessels, around the time of the Napoleonic Wars, arranged their cannonballs in a pyramid on a brass plate called a 'monkey', and that in cold weather the cannonballs would contract and and fall off this 'monkey'. However, there is no record of such a plate having been in use, or such an arrangement of cannonballs onboard a sea-faring vessel.

Actually, in the nineteenth century, the term 'brass monkey' was widely used in other ways. *The Story of Waitstill Baxter* (1913), by Kate Douglas Wiggin, included the line 'The little feller, now, is smart's a whip, an' could talk the tail off a brass monkey.' It was even used to describe hot weather, as in Herman Melville's *Omoo* (1850): 'To use a hyperbolical phrase of Shorty's, "It was 'ot enough to melt the nose h'off a brass monkey."'

So, its most likely origin stems from the image of a brass statue being emasculated, illustrating extremes of temperature; that the heat or cold is so great that it could even affect such a solid and seemingly unbreakable object.

'Taking the mickey'

Although this seems like the polite version of 'taking the piss', it actually means exactly the same thing – and has nothing to do with anyone called Michael. When the word 'piss' became regarded as offensive, the phrase changed to 'taking the micturations', where 'micturate' means 'to urinate'. It was later shortened to 'taking the mickey'.

The Neologisms; Or, The New Ones That Someone Made Up

'Fug'

In his book *The Naked and the Dead*, Norman Mailer invented this euphemism for 'fuck'. When introduced to American critic and wit Dorothy Parker at a party, she quipped, 'So you're the young man who can't spell "fuck"?'

'Naff off'

Famously used by the usually aristocratic Princess Anne, 'naff off' was brought into popular use by the seventies' sitcom *Porridge* starring Ronnie Barker. Even though it was a comedy, the absence of swear words in a show about hardened criminals would have been too divorced from reality; unfortunately, the television audiences of the time were not ready for the type of language normally heard in Her Majesty's prisons. To get round this dilemma the writers, Dick Clement and Ian La Frenais, used 'naff' as Fletcher's favourite expletive, usually as 'naff off' or 'naffing'.

The origin of the term 'naff' is thought by some to have come from an acronym meaning 'nasty as fuck'; equally, it could also have come from the military slang of the Second World War, where 'SNAFU' apparently stood for 'Situation Normal – All Fucked Up'.

In some gay circles the word is now used as an insult to heterosexuals – meaning 'not a fucking fairy'!

'Nadgers'

Like 'bollocks', 'nadgers' can be used as an exclamation ('oh nadgers!') or can refer to testicles. Terry Pratchett's book *Maskerade*, for example, includes the line: 'There was no point freezing your nadgers off on top of some mountain while communing with the Infinite unless you could rely on a lot of impressionably young women to come along occasionally and say "Gosh".'

The word first surfaced in the 1950s on *The Goon Show* and was used as a general nonsense word in a few sketches, including the introduction to the song 'Eeh! Ah! Oh! Ooh!', which boasted the wonderful line: 'Doctors strongly recommend it as a cure for the lurgi, the onset of the nadgers, spots before the ankles, soft shoulders, pink toenails and acute [something unintelligible] of the legs.'

Ten years later, *Round the Horne* star Kenneth Williams used 'nadgers' when playing Rambling Syd Rumpo, a regular character who replaced words in traditional song with suggestive-sounding nonsense. In a corruption of the title line from 'What Shall We Do With a Drunken Sailor?' he sang the line, 'Hit him in the nadgers with the bosun's plunger.'

The word has several close relations in the English language and could have been a corruption of the one or more words that are already used to refer to male genitals; i.e. 'gonads' or 'knackers', both meaning testicles, and 'tadger', meaning penis.

'Smeg'

Writer Grant Naylor used the word 'smeg' as a general expletive in his 1988 sci-fi sitcom *Red Dwarf*, starring Craig Charles. The similarity to the word 'smegma', meaning a secretion in the folds of the skin (especially under a man's foreskin), has led many to assume that it is a contraction of the word.

Naylor also invented the futuristic insults 'goit' and 'gimboid', and also made use of the word 'nadgers'.

Cockney Curses; Or, Swear Words in Rhyming Slang

Since the mid-nineteenth century, those born within the sound of Bow bells have been getting away with words that others wouldn't dare utter, using rhyming slang. The following is a list of dirty cockney rhyming slang.

> Artful Dodger – Todger
> Billy Bragg – Shag
> Bristol City – Titty
> Clement Freud – Haemorrhoid
> Elephant and Castle – Arsehole
> Elizabeth Fringe – Minge
> Friar Tuck – Fuck
> Gravel and Grit – Shit
> Jackson Pollocks – Bollocks
> Jodrell Bank – Wank
> Kate Moss – Toss
> Orphan Annie – Fanny

American Abuse; Or, Lost in Translation

Oscar Wilde once described Britain and America as 'two nations divided by a common language.' Despite the increasingly shared culture of the two countries, the division is still quite evident when it comes to foul language.

What means 'bottom' to an Englishman means 'a vagrant' to an American, while the word that Americans use for 'bottom' refers to something completely different on this side of the Atlantic.

Inadvertently highlighting these discrepancies, American soul group The Tams released a song in 1987 called 'There Ain't Nothing Like Shaggin''. To the American market it was a song about the latest dance craze. Although it reached the No. 21 in the UK charts, it had a lot of trouble getting airplay as, understandably, British broadcasters and listeners thought it was about another activity altogether!

'Bum'

In the UK, the word is a pretty acceptable word for the posterior, for which the US equivalent is 'butt'. In the US, a 'bum' is a hobo or a tramp. It can also be used to mean 'to borrow', as in 'Can I bum a light?' – although the phrase 'Can I bum a fag?' should probably be used with caution on either side of the Atlantic!

'Fanny'

To an American the word 'fanny' also means the backside, and is as harmless as saying 'butt'. To the British population the word is more offensive and refers to the female genitals. In the 1970s, a US all-girl band called Wild Honey were advised by the Beatles' George Harrison to change their name to Fanny, which they duly did. Unfortunately, what George apparently neglected to tell them was the meaning of the word to the UK market. What a wag!

'Willy'

This euphemism for the male member is totally lost on the Americans. Why else would they release a children's film about a whale and call it *Free Willy*? To a UK audience it sounds less like an instruction to release a whale than a special offer for sex-starved women.

'Wank'

'Wank' and 'wanker' are peculiarly British terms and mean nothing to Americans. Although the term 'wanker' has appeared in TV shows such as *Buffy the Vampire Slayer* and *ER*, it has

Derivation: 'Bloody'

a) adverb – to quantify something as extreme

Popular theory has it that this mild invective is a corruption of the blasphemous phrase 'by Our Lady', which accounts for why it was excised from printed works from the mid-eighteenth century even until, in some cases, the early twentieth century. According to language expert Geoffrey Hughes, however, this derivation does not work, as the phrase 'by Our Lady' does not fit in with the sentences in which we would use 'bloody'. You could not say, for example, 'by Our Lady hell!', and 'it is by Our Lady cold today' doesn't make much sense either. Instead, he believes, the word is more literally exactly as it sounds and comes from the word 'bloody' as in 'fiery' or 'spirited'. 'Bloods' was also the name used to describe young and rowdy British aristocrats of the seventeenth and eighteenth centuries, and thus being 'bloody drunk' suggests being 'as drunk as a blood'.

always been spoken by a Brit and is not a word you are likely to hear from an American actor in a Hollywood film. Surprisingly, the word was used twice in *The Simpsons* episode 'The Trash of the Titans', which featured guest stars U2. The censors originally allowed it because its viewers wouldn't understand it. On British television it was dubbed out, but was later shown in a post-watershed slot. A popular US euphemism for masturbation is

'Bloody' is almost never heard in America, while being extremely common in the UK and Australia. Identified by Francis Grose in his *A Classical Dictionary of the Vulgar Tongue* as 'a favourite word used by thieves in swearing', it is not surprising that the 160,000 convicts who were shipped to Australia from Britain between 1788 and 1868 took the word with them.

Alexander Marjoribanks, in his 1847 *Travels in New South Wales*, commented that a bullock driver used the word twenty-seven times in fifteen minutes. Amazed at the frequency of the oath, he calculated that, over a fifty-year period, the man would have used 'this disgusting word no less than 18,200,000 times'.

Although seen as mild and inoffensive today, 'bloody' was once regarded as a shocking word, and in 1914 its inclusion in a West End stage play caused national outrage (see pages 66-7), and became known as 'the Shavian adjective'. Because of this it has spawned several euphemisms, including 'blooming', 'blinking', 'ruddy' and 'bleeding'.

Variations include: bloody hell, bloody-minded

'jerk off' (which can be used as either a noun, to refer to a person, or as a verb, to refer to the act itself), which sounds almost civil. Unlike 'wank', which tends to apply to male masturbation, 'jerking off' can be done by men or women.

Famous Foul-mouths: No Laughing Matter

Live comedy has always been an arena for the filthiest of language. Long before it was considered respectable to swear on TV, stand-up comedians performing in theatres, clubs, or on video could let their mouths run, safe in the knowledge that those listening would not be offended because they were likely to be fans.

A curious effect of the regulations of TV broadcasting, however, meant that for many years plenty of well-known comedians, such as Jim Davidson and Mike Reid, lived double lives – as cuddly presenters on TV and foul-mouthed entertainers on stage. This section celebrates a few of the most infamous foul-mouthed funnymen of recent times.

Max Miller

To British audiences of the 1950s, Max Miller's routines were considered somewhat risqué. The music-hall star and original 'cheeky chappy' always offered his audience a choice of the white joke book (respectable) or the blue joke book (dirty). Invariably, the crowd would call for the blue book. And, of course, he was happy to give the audience what they wanted.

One gag in particular got Miller in hot water, and caused not a little controversy:

I was walking along this narrow mountain pass – so narrow that nobody else could pass you, when I saw a beautiful blonde walking towards me. A beautiful blonde with not a stitch on, yes, not a stitch on, lady. Cor blimey, I didn't know whether to toss myself off or block her passage.

Many claim that Max once told this joke on the radio and was 'faded out' before he got to the punch line (presumably by someone who knew what was coming!) and, although the joke is contained in the *The Max Miller Appreciation Society's Blue Book,* there is some doubt as to whether he ever told it. The actor Roy Hudd, an aficionado of classic comedy, claimed on the TV documentary *Heroes of Comedy* that he did not believe that Max would ever have told the joke as he would have thought it too bawdy and not subtle enough.

But Leslie Irons, co-compiler of the *MMASBB*, believes that it was this joke that got Max banned from BBC radio for five years. He claims that Max certainly knew the joke as he was heard to say, 'They should not have faded me out because I was not going to use that ending'; Irons also claims to remember the controversy at the time.

Another contributor to the *Max Miller Appreciation Society*'s website agrees. Ronald Jones, of Melbourne in Australia, said, 'I am positive that I heard Max get cut off the air when he told the joke about blocking the passage. I remember it vividly because when I went out to play the other kids were asking each other had they heard it on the radio. And it was gossip for a while in school, not that we really understood it, as we were really innocent in them days.' Probably for the best!

Billy Connolly

Billy Connolly grew up in the tenements of Glasgow and spent his teens as an apprentice in a shipyard on the River Clyde. Not surprisingly, the language of the streets is a permanent presence in his comedy routines.

Connolly's big break came on the talk-show, *Parkinson* when he told a risqué joke about a hard-up Glaswegian who murdered his wife and buried her with her arse sticking out of the ground so that he would have 'somewhere to park his bike'. Parky looked nervous and the BBC were expecting complaints, but the 'Big Yin' managed to pull it off (as it were), and he rapidly became one of the most popular comedy stars of his era, both as a live performer and on TV in his *Billy Connolly's World Tour* . . . series.

In 2003, he received the royal seal of approval when he was awarded a CBE. Initially taking some pride in the fact that he'd avoided swearing throughout the royal-studded ceremony at Buckingham Palace, Connolly's self-imposed self-restraint didn't last long. When a photographer reached out to touch the precious award, Billy protested loudly, 'Get the fuck away from my medal. Fuck off.'

In *Billy*, her biography of her husband, his wife Pamela Stephenson wrote: 'At his funeral, he hopes aeroplanes will zoom overhead writing "Fuck the Begrudgers!" in the sky. This saying has always been a consoling mantra for him. Every time he has a great concert but is wailed at in the papers, he repeats it to remind himself to shrug the feelings off.' He has also advised his wife that his epigraph on his gravestone is to be 'Jesus Christ, is that the time already?'

'The only other gravestone inscription he would settle for is tiny writing in the middle of a huge stone,' she says. 'The writing should be so small that people would have to get up really close to read: "You're standing on my balls."'

In one hilarious routine, Billy describes some of the things he hates about everyone – here are some extracts:

People who point at their wrist while asking for the time . . . I know where my watch is pal, where the fuck is yours? Do I point at my crotch when I ask where the toilet is?

When people say, 'Oh, you just want to have your cake and eat it too!' Fucking right! What good is a cake if you can't eat it?

When people say while watching a film, 'Did you see that?' No tosser, I paid ten quid to come to the cinema and stare at the fucking floor.

When people say, 'Life is short.' What the fuck? Life is the longest damn thing anyone ever fucking does! What can you do that's longer?

When you are waiting for the bus and someone asks, 'Has the bus come yet?' If the bus came would I be standing here, knobhead?

McDonalds staff who pretend they don't understand you if you don't insert the 'Mc' before the item you are ordering . . . It has to be a McChicken Burger. Just a Chicken Burger gets blank looks. Well, I'll have a McStraw and jam it in your McEyes, you fucking McTosser.

Roy 'Chubby' Brown

Roy 'Chubby' Brown is the self-proclaimed 'crudest and rudest' comedian around, and he's proud of it. The Middlesbrough-born comic is unlikely to appear on many daytime shows, although he did make it on to *Top of the Pops* after recording 'Living Next Door to Alice (Who the Fuck is Alice?)' with Smokie. Apparently, when Smokie used to play in Ireland and the band would sing the title lyric, their audience would shout back 'Who the fuck is Alice?' So Smokie asked Roy to record with them a spoof of their own song and it was an instant hit. 'I'm the first bloke ever in the charts with a song with "fuck" in it,' says Roy proudly.

After various jobs, including scaffolder, cook and waiter, Roy (whose real name is Royston Vasey, *League of Gentlemen* fans . . .) joined a band and toured working men's clubs. Following an appearance on *Opportunity Knocks* where he lost the competition to a spoon player, his manager suggested he should 'go completely blue', as clean comedians were ten a penny. According to his website he had difficulty with the swearing at first, but then grew into the role quite easily. 'I decided to go right over the top and be the rudest man in the country and I haven't looked back,' says the rudest man in the country.

Signs outside his live show say 'If easily offended, stay away', his videos and tapes carry an 18 certificate and have titles like *Thunder Bollocks*, *Jingle Bollocks*, *Saturday Night Beaver* and the slightly cleverer *Obscene but not Heard*. Even his website carries a warning: 'By the very nature of Chubby's act some people may be offended by the content of this site. If you think you may be one of those people, do not enter.'

Believe it or not, Roy, whose trademark outfit is a pair of goggles and a flying hat, has *some* sensibilities. His late mother was banned from seeing his act, as are his grandchildren. 'I hate swearing in front of women and kids off the stage,' he says. 'I don't think there's any need for it. I try to keep my family values and if I hear someone effing and blinding in the street I give them a look.'

Derivation: 'Frig'

a) verb – to masturbate
b) verb – to copulate
c) noun – an act of masturbation

Often used as, supposedly, a more polite way of saying the F-word, 'frig' has come to mean 'to copulate', although its original meaning was 'to masturbate'.

It derives from the Middle English meaning 'wriggle' and the Old French for 'rub', and, according to Farmer and Henley's definitive work, *Slang and its Analogues* (1890–1904), had its first use in 1598 by John Florio (in *A World of Words*) who defined the word 'friccaire' as 'to frig, to wriggle, to tickle.' In 1785 Francis Grose, in his *A Classical Dictionary of the Vulgar Tongue*, defined 'to frig' as, 'To be guilty of the crime of self-pollution. The word is often seen as a gerundive, as in "frigging"'.

Variations include: frigging hell, frick, fricking

This proved to be his undoing when he came face to face with fan Edward McCullough in Blackpool in 2003. Mr McCullough shouted out, 'How are you, Chubby? How are you, you fat bastard?' whereupon Roy hit him with an umbrella. Mr Brown claimed he 'just wanted the man to stop swearing and being abusive in front of women and children'. But he lost the case and was fined £200 and ordered to pay £150 in costs and compensation.

It's a funny old world!

Mike Reid

To the younger generation he is known as Frank in *EastEnders*, but before he took up residence in Albert Square Mike Reid had a long and successful career as a stand-up comedian.

Born in Hackney in 1940, Reid grew up determined to break into the world of entertainment and worked as a movie stuntman while he awaited his breakthrough on the comedy circuit. In the early seventies, a variety show called *The Comedians* made him a household name and in 1975 he landed a job as the presenter of the kids' TV quiz show *Runaround*. *The Mike Reid Show* followed in 1976, and for a short period the cockney comic was everybody's favourite family entertainer.

Fans who came to see his live shows, however, saw another side of Mike Reid – and it certainly wasn't for kids. The routines were laced with the F-word and the humour was often smutty. A typical Mike Reid gag (for his *Alive and Kicking* tour) went: 'Quasimodo's running down the boulevard pursued by twenty school kids. He finally turns around and yells, "For once and for all, I don't have your fucking football!"'

Another: 'Two nuns are driving through Transylvania, and Dracula suddenly appears and climbs onto their windshield. One turns to the other and says, "Show him your cross." So the nun gets out and yells to Dracula, "Get off the fucking car!"'

In 1994 Mike starred in an adult pantomime called *Pussy In Boots* with *EastEnders* co-stars John Altman and Barbara Windsor. His own character was called – you guessed it – Big Dick Whittington. Ten years on, in 2004, he released his latest video and DVD, *Seriously Funny*, and just so you are in no doubt as to whether there's any swearing in it – it has an 18 certificate.

Fucking
Fascinating
Facts

**Wherein is contained certain
anecdotes, facts, news items and
other miscellanea about the joys of
swearing ...**

Fancy Living There!

In the ancient British tradition of naming streets and roads after the activities and trades that thrived there, both Oxford and London once had a Gropecunte Lane. Unsurprisingly, the road was renowned for its prostitutes. The Oxford locale was later renamed Magpie Lane, while London's Gropecunte Lane, a small lane off Cheapside in the City, is thought to be the modern day Threadneedle Street.

Similarly, we could surmise that there may have been prostitutes catering for a different market in the nearby streets of Cock's Lane and Lad Lane.

Sherborne Lane, near Cannon Street, was originally Shiteburn Lane, meaning 'shit house' – which once upon a time housed public lavatories. Lillian Road in Barnes used to be called Fanny Road, but the sign was stolen so many times that the despairing council had to change the name.

World Place Names To Snigger At

Bald Knob, Arkansas

Chinaman's Knob, Australia

Crap, Albania

Cunt, Turkey

Dildo Island, Newfoundland, Canada – the largest of three islands located at the entrance to Dildo Arm, off the coast of the neighbouring town of Dildo.

Fucking, Austria – the sign on entering the town reads 'Fucking: Please, not so fast.' That's a passionate plea for you.

Fuku, China

Knob Lick, Missouri

Middelfart, Denmark

Pis Pis River, Nicaragua

Pussy, France

The Dirty Dozen of UK Place Names

Bell End, Worcestershire (near Lickey End)

Bonar Bridge, Inverness

Cockermouth, Cumbria

Pishill, Oxfordshire

Pratt's Bottom, Kent

Prickwillow, Cambridgeshire

Slaggyford, Northumberland

Titsey, Surrey

Twatt, villages on both the isles of Orkney and Shetland

Upper Dicker, East Sussex (near Lower Dicker)

Upper Thong, West Yorkshire

Wetwang, East Yorkshire

What's In a Name?

Bizarrely, *fukt* means 'humidity' in mainstream Swedish. You can also buy 'Fukt Creme' in some shops in Sweden.

Sweden and Denmark are a rich source of rude brand names. As well as 'Fukt Creme' you can find cat food called 'Pussi Favorit', chocolate bars called 'Plopps' and 'Käck', and candies called 'Spunk'. The latter come in two flavours: wine-gum flavour, and salted anchovy flavour, which gives rise to the eternal dilemma – spit or swallow.

The name of the Welsh village in Dylan Thomas's masterpiece *Under Milk Wood* is 'Llareggub'. When asked what it meant, Thomas suggested that the name be read backwards!

France boasts a restaurant that serves crêpes and pizzas and revels in the name 'Crep 'n' Pizz'.

Fucking Unlucky!

In 2000, UK resident Balraj Gill made history when he was arrested for swearing at police – in sign language!

The officers had taken the deaf man back to the Lancashire hostel where he was staying and, although they knew he was agitated, they had no idea what Mr Gill was trying to say to them. It wasn't until an obliging worker at the hostel translated every word to the astounded officers that they realized he was hurling abuse at them, albeit silently.

The worker's translation landed the unlucky curser in court in Blackburn where, despite the quiet nature of his profanities, he admitted breaching the peace.

Parrots and Profanity

In 2004, it was reported that Winston Churchill's pet parrot, Charlie, was alive and well and living at a garden centre in Surrey. The parrot, who was 104 and was said to have been at Churchill's side throughout the war years, was entertaining visitors to the nursery with anti-Nazi slogans learnt, apparently, from the famous politician.

Her favourite curses were 'Fuck Hitler' and 'Fuck the Nazis'.

Owner Peter Oram claimed that Churchill bought the blue-and-gold macaw in 1937 and kept her at Chartwell, once Churchill's Westerham home, where the war leader taught her the language of the trenches.

The Churchill family, however, have questioned Mr Oram's story, and historians have said they are unsure if the leader ever owned a parrot.

●

A saucy squawker was sacked from his role in a pantomime in 1999 after swearing during rehearsals. Percy, an Amazonian green parrot, was supposed to star as the pirates' parrot in a Christmas production of *Pirates on Treasure Island,* for the Jakes Ladder Theatre Company in Blandford, Dorset. But in the final run-through Percy decided to improvise by replacing the line 'pieces of eight' with the less traditional 'piss off, mate'. At first the cast overlooked the faux pas, but Percy hadn't finished. He took to chanting 'bugger off, bugger off' before moving on to a few stronger words.

Managers decided they could not risk the foul-beaked parrot offending young members of the audience, and they sacked him. He's since been dropped by his agent.

More Fascinating Facts

In 1649, the British Parliament introduced the death penalty for swearing at one's parents, a statute which, were it revived today, would surely wipe out an entire generation.

Since unparliamentary language is banned in New Zealand's House of Representatives, as it is in the UK, MPs have used their imagination to insult their opposite numbers while sticking to the rules. However, spotting this trend, Speakers in the 1930s set up a compendium of 'unparliamentary language'. The following phrases appear in the indexes of the *New Zealand Parliamentary Debates* and show the sort of insults that members of the house have attempted to get away with. They are a fascinating record not only of the ingenious lengths to which politicians would go to make their point, but they also give an insight into a range of different historical insults.

1933   'Blow-fly minded'
                  'Financial Frankenstein'
                  'Shrewd old bird'

1936   'Fungus farmer'
                  'Pipsqueak'

1943   'Retardate worm'

1946   'Clown of the House'
                  'Idle vapourings of a mind diseased'
                  'I would cut the honourable gentleman's
                      throat if I had the chance'
                  'Quasi-parsonical'
                  'Skite'

1949	'His brains could revolve inside a peanut shell for a thousand years without touching the sides' 'Hoey' 'Hypnotized rabbits'
1957	'Kind of animal that gnaws holes' 'Trained seals'
1959	'Member not fit to lick the shoes of the Prime Minister'
1963	'Energy of a tired snail returning home from a funeral' 'Sits on his behind'
1966	'Shut up yourself, you great ape' 'Snotty nosed little boy' 'You are a cheap little twerp' 'Ridiculous mouse'
1969	'Duck shoving' 'Like a snail leaves a slime behind him'
1974	'Scuttles for his political funk hole' 'Could go down the Mount Eden sewer and come up cleaner than he went in' 'Dreamed the Bill up in the bath' 'Greasy hands' 'Grubby little man' 'Intestinal fortitude' 'Mealy mouthed 'Slinking off to another part of the House' 'Frustrated warlord'

1977	'John Boy'
	'Silly old moo'
	'Sober up'
1980	'Ayatollah'
	'Ditch the bitch'
	'Fascist dictator'
	'Marxist or neo-Marxist'

In 2005, a sample of a teacher swearing at his class was put to a techno beat and became a surprise hit on Belgian radio. Professor Yves De Racker, a maths teacher at Karel de Grote High School in Antwerp, was cursing at his students when one of them recorded his voice and a friend added a dance beat. They then e-mailed the track to a pal who sent it to the local youth radio station, which played it on air.

While the school refused to condone the language, Vice Dean Anne Goffin said, 'They are all big boys and sometimes it is not easy to attract their attention. Every teacher has his own way of teaching and Prof. De Racker has been in the army for a long time.'

Radio presenter Peter Van de Veire said, 'We were amazed by the huge response of the listeners who thought they recognized their former teacher in the Racker Song.' Prof De Racker kept his expletives to himself when told about the song. 'I'm very glad my students were able to make a sample like that,' he said. 'I don't think many colleagues can boast of having their own song.'

●

The phrase 'Pardon my French', used as an apology when a swear word has slipped out or been deemed as necessary even when it might cause offence, was first used in *Harper's Magazine* in 1895. The reason the French language was singled out for the phrase is that, at the time, the French were associated with all things vulgar. As far back as the early sixteenth century, 'French

Derivation: 'Prat'

a) noun – a stupid or idiotic person

The word 'prat' has had a varied existence and three different meanings throughout its lifetime. In the sixteenth century it was a common word for 'buttocks' or 'backside'. By the nineteenth century it had come to mean 'vagina', and, in modern-day vernacular, it is most commonly used to mean 'an idiot'.

The first meaning above gave us the word 'pratfall', meaning to fall on one's arse.

In the US, in the early years of the twentieth century, a 'prat' was a hip-pocket and a 'prat digger' was a term for a pickpocket.

Variations include: prat about

pox' and the 'French disease' were synonyms for genital herpes, and 'French-sick' was another term for syphilis. The adjective 'French' has long been associated with all things risqué, which accounts for 'French letter' (a condom), 'French kiss' (first used around 1923) and 'French novels' (books with sexually explicit content).

More Celebrity Swearing

One of the most dignified doyennes of the British screen, Dame Judi Dench, has a decidedly wicked streak. 'I have this devilish hobby of embroidering naughty needlework for the directors when I make movies,' she explained. 'I give them these intricate, delicate tapestries, and the cushions include expletives that can't be easily seen at first.'

David Hare was one person who fell foul of her little tricks. Knowing she was good at needlepoint, Hare asked Dame Judi to make something for him to give his mum on Mother's Day. Dame Judi presented him with the gift and the embroidery was beautiful. It was only after he'd given it to his mum that he noticed the words 'Fuck off' stitched into the material. Perhaps Dame Judi should call her unusual hobby 'embrudery'?

In 1974, as a British tour drew to an end, singing duo The Carpenters sent music industry executives gifts as a memento. Each one received a tiny velvet box containing a gold ring. Inscribed on one side of the ring was the word 'love'. On the other side was the word 'fuck'.

Heather Graham was banned from starring in the aptly named *Heathers* because her parents thought it was 'dirty and disgusting'. She told *Movieline* magazine that her strictly Catholic mother and father stopped their teenage daughter from taking the role after reading one particular line. The offending line? 'Fuck me gently with a chainsaw.' Perhaps they had a point!

W. C. Fields was renowned for his sharp tongue and irascible nature. In order to stop himself from using unprintable language while venting his spleen, however, he invented his own set of swear words which were delivered in such a way that they sounded every bit as threatening as the original expletives. His favourite curse was 'Godfrey Daniel!' and it apparently sounded so vulgar that audiences couldn't understand how the censors allowed it.

●

According to the *San Francisco Examiner*, it was handbags at dawn when fashion designer Calvin Klein came face to face with bitchy comedienne Joan Rivers at the 2002 Cannes Film Festival. Seated together at a dinner, Klein, annoyed by Joan's constant banter, shouted across the table, 'You're a cunt. You're nothing but an old cunt, you cunt!' Proving that his vocabulary is not as varied as his couture.

Reportedly, Elton John and Liz Taylor, who were also at the table, were stunned, but Joan didn't hear him. Her daughter Melissa eventually told her mother what Klein had called her, and so Joan approached the designer and said, 'Excuse me. Melissa said you called me a cunt.' Calvin replied, 'I sure did and your daughter's an even uglier cunt.' Unfortunately, he spoiled his dramatic exit when he tripped over while trying to storm out of the room! Content – 9, Style – 0!

Did You Hear the One About . . . ?

(A few good jokes to leave you laughing)

> *Mary had a little skirt*
> *With splits right up the sides*
> *And every time that Mary walked*
> *The boys could see her thighs*
> *Mary had another skirt*
> *It was split right up the front*
> *. . . But she didn't wear that one very often*

●

A magazine launches a competition for the rudest poem in the world and is amazed when the prize is won by a little old lady.

Spotting a great story, the reporters turn up at her door and when the little old lady answers they ask her to recite it.

'But I can't,' she says. 'You won't be able to print it.'

'I know,' says one reporter. 'Just replace all the really rude words with "dum-de-dum" and we'll work out the rest.'

'OK,' says the old lady, and off she goes.

'Dum-de-dum-de-dum-de-dum

Dum-de-dum-de-dum

Dum-de-dum-de-dum-de-dum

Dum-de-dum-de-dum

Dum-de-dum-de-dum-de-dum

Dum-de-dum-de-dum

Dum-de-dum-de-dum-de-dum

Dum-de-dum-de-CUNT!'

●

In 2003, Dustin Hoffman appeared on Channel Four's *V Graham Norton* and told the following joke:

Johnny is nine years old. He's got a train set for his Christmas present and he's playing with it in the living room. His mother is in the kitchen cooking and she hears 'Brooooooom! All aboard for San Francisco. Anyone getting off, get the fuck off. Anyone getting on, get the fuck on.'

Mum thinks, 'I can't believe what I'm hearing,' then she hears 'Brooooooom! All aboard for Los Angeles. Anyone getting off, get the fuck off. Anyone getting on, get the fuck on.'

Mum drops what she's doing, storms out of the kitchen and says, 'Johnny, that was a Christmas present. I can't believe what is coming out of your mouth. It has nothing to do with anything we have ever taught you. Go upstairs and stand in the corner for an hour.'

Johnny goes upstairs, and an hour and twenty minutes later his mother hears 'Brooooooom! All aboard for San Diego. Anyone getting off, get off. Anyone getting on, get on . . . And if you want to know why the train is over an hour late, ask the cunt in the kitchen.'

Sadly, the TV watchdogs weren't laughing. The Broadcasting Standards Commission condemned the use of the C-word and found that the word had 'potential for serious offence to viewers', and therefore 'crossed acceptable boundaries'. Never mind, Dustin – it was a bloody good joke!

Conclusion

Shortly before writing this, I happened to hear a man, in his thirties, having a loud conversation on his mobile phone in the quiet village in which I live.

'I don't give a shit,' the guy was saying. '*You* don't fucking have to live with her. I want her to fucking leave me alone and stay out of my fucking life. She won't fucking leave me alone.'

In the next breath he said, 'You've got to stop doing this, Mum!'

The most shocking word in that sentence, to me, was 'Mum'. The words he chose to express his anger are in everyday use, but the realization that he was talking to his mum and *still* using those words amazed me.

The fact is that the vast majority of swear words are no longer taboo. As time has passed, their use in the street, on films, on TV and radio, in literature and music has become largely accepted – the only sticking point is the context in which they are used. The F-word is not for your mum, for instance, but in the course of a conversation with your mates for many it has become a natural part of speech.

A hundred years ago the word 'bloody' could cause a national outcry, and seventy years ago 'damn' in a Hollywood film had a director fighting with the censors. Fifty years ago men would swear, but never in front of a lady – but the drive toward sexual equality and the birth of the 'ladette' put paid to that polite convention. Even twenty years ago 'fuck' was still shocking, and 'cunt' was absolutely taboo, rare in films and unheard of on TV.

Our relationship with swearing, profanity, blasphemy, puerile language, vulgarity, vituperation, oaths, cusses and foul-mouthed language has been a long and rich one. Each word in turn has riled us, and then receded; risen in notoriety and then waned through overuse. They provide us with the necessary vocabulary to utter our immediate and instinctive feelings of anger, annoyance, pain, disappointment and despair. And they are also our reference points toward the taboo, allowing us to mention what can't be mentioned straight on, and giving us the opportunity to couch our thoughts in ways that may be humorous, wicked, or just plain rude. The future of swearing is the future of both language and culture – all three are intrinsically intertwined, and where they all may go is a mystery. In the meantime, I leave you with a joke, a perfect example of the way we use bad language today.

A man is talking to his friend about a girl he met the night before.

'I went to the fucking pub and saw this fucking beautiful girl. I thought, "Fucking hell, she's fucking gorgeous."'

'What happened then?' asks his friend.

'I bought her a fucking drink and started fucking talking to her,' he says.

'What happened then?' asks his friend again.

'She said she wanted to leave, so we tried to get a fucking cab but fucking ended up walking all the way to her fucking flat. Then she asked me in for a fucking drink.'

'What happened then?'

'We made love.'

Sources

Ayto, John,
The Oxford Dictionary of Slang
(Oxford University Press, 2003)

Haver, Ronald,
David O. Selznick's Hollywood
(Outlet, 1985)

Hughes, Geoffrey,
Swearing
(Penguin Books, 1998)

Lewis, Chris,
The Dictionary of Playground Slang
(Allison and Busby, 2003)

Sheidlower, Jesse,
The F-Word
(Random House, 1999)

Smith, Anthony (ed.),
Television: An International History
(Oxford University Press, 1995)